The Ways of Wildfowl

All day thy wings have fann'd,
At that far height, the cold thin atmos-
     phere;
Yet stoop not, weary, to the welcome
     land,
    Though the dark night is near.

And soon that toil shall end,
Soon shalt thou find a summer home, and
     rest,
And scream among thy fellows; reeds
     shall bend,
    Soon, o'er thy sheltered nest.

from TO A WATERFOWL
by William Cullen Bryant

The Ways of Wildfowl

FEATURING THE DISTINGUISHED
PAINTINGS AND ETCHINGS OF

with text by Russ Williams

Edited by Thomas C. Jones

Published by

J. G. FERGUSON PUBLISHING COMPANY / CHICAGO

Distributed to the book trade by
DOUBLEDAY & COMPANY / NEW YORK

ACKNOWLEDGMENTS

The etchings and paintings of Richard E. Bishop have been internationally acclaimed for thirty-five years. Countless days and nights in fields, forests, flowages, and duck blinds with a movie camera and a sketch pad have given him firsthand knowledge of the actions and habits of the wildfowl his paintings glorify. His miles of movie film, slowed to one-eighth speed, reveal flight acrobatics imperceptible to the human eye and amazing to wildlife authorities and aeronautical engineers alike.

Richard Bishop's interest in wildfowl stems from the days of his boyhood when he tramped the uplands or sat patiently in a blind on a marsh with his father. He attended Cornell University and earned an engineering degree. By 1920 he was embarked on a successful business career as the superintendent of a rolling mill. It was about this time that he idly scratched an image on a piece of scrap copper and discovered a new and fascinating hobby — etching. A few years later, his famous *Canada Geese* won the Charles M. Lea Prize and he gave up the rolling-mill work to earn his living as a professional artist and craftsman.

In 1936 the United States government commissioned him to design the migratory bird hunting stamp. *Coming In,* showing three Canada geese, was the painting that became the design for the stamp of that year.

This master etcher, craftsman, and artist has turned out hundreds of paintings and etchings that have delighted lovers of outdoor sport and waterfowl. Reproductions of Mr. Bishop's paintings have appeared on fine glassware and service plates, as well as on exclusive calendars.

Books featuring Bishop's work have twice been produced in limited editions. In 1936 an edition of seventy-three of his etchings was produced by the J. B. Lippincott Company under the title *Bishop's Birds, Etchings of Waterfowl and Upland Game Birds.*

Twelve years later, *Bishop's Wildfowl* was published by the well-known advertising firm, Brown & Bigelow. The coauthor of that volume, Russ Williams, is the author of this work.

As a result of the cooperation of Richard E. Bishop, Russ Williams, Brown & Bigelow, Photopress, Inc., and many dedicated individuals with each of these firms, it has been possible to include in this volume a total of sixty-four reproductions of color paintings together with many etchings that constitute a representative selection of Bishop's work.

The text by Russ Williams has a lyrical quality that matches the physical beauty of the illustrations. The exciting spirit of the outdoors comes alive through the graceful prose that introduces the various species of wildfowl.

We are indebted to the United States Department of the Interior, Fish and Wildlife Service, for permission to reproduce maps of the flyways and a number of illustrations by the noted wildlife artist, Bob Hines. Also, we appreciate the permission to reproduce several illustrations from the excellent volume, *Prairie Wings,* by Edgar M. Queeny. Likewise, we wish to recognize the extraordinary dedication and cooperation of many individuals whose work has made this volume possible — my assistant, Harriet Helmer, designer Al Josephson and the entire Photopress organization, the Poole-Clarinda Company, Chicago, the Brown & Bigelow Creative Department, and the Engdahl Company, book bindery at Elmhurst, Illinois.

We feel very fortunate in having the opportunity to participate in a project that ties in so directly with the national and worldwide interest in preserving our precious heritage of natural beauty and the miracles of the world of wildfowl. The colorful and scientifically accurate work of Richard E. Bishop combined with the extraordinary talent of Russ Williams to tell the story in such appealing style have merged to create a volume that will fascinate many readers.

Thomas C. Jones

INTRODUCTION

Have you ever looked up into the sky on a soft spring night when the moon was full and thrilled to the glorious gabbling of high-flying geese moving northward? And wondered at the strange power of their primordial chorus to grip the heart with a restless yearning for the wild freedom of the wilderness and far-away places? If you have, you know that the world of wildfowl is truly a wonder-filled universe of beautiful, fascinating, and amazing creatures—a world rich in rewarding experience for all who delight in exploring this winged realm of beauty and sound.

The inestimable value of our wildfowl—and all forms of wildlife—has now been brought into sharp focus by our environmental crisis. In the last year alone the wildlife species on the official endangered list has jumped from 89 to 102! The possibility that whole populations of birds and wildfowl will soon be wiped out is very real. Actually, it is in process. We are presently witnessing the terrifying effect of pesticides and herbicides that are polluting waters inhabited by wildlife of all kinds.

Hopefully, *The Ways of Wildfowl* will bring—especially to young people—a deeper appreciation of the God-given legacy we have in our wildfowl and all living things upon this earth. This is not a scientific work or a textbook. It is an informal collection of stories about ducks, geese, and other species of wildfowl in North America, featuring an unusual and priceless presentation of superb paintings and etchings by one of America's most popular wildfowl artists, Richard E. Bishop.

In the years that I have known Richard Bishop, he has held an affectionate place, not only in my heart but also in the hearts of sportsmen and bird lovers everywhere who cherish the sensitive quality of his artistry. Never before has such an extensive gallery of his paintings and etchings been presented in book form. With a rare talent for not only painting and etching, but also for photographic research and field study, Richard Bishop possesses a vast and intimate knowledge of wildfowl—a knowledge gleaned from years of tramping in the woods, fields, and swamps of North America with motion-picture camera and easel. Among other things, he has filmed slow-motion pictures of teal flying upside

down. His studio contains one of the world's most extensive color film libraries, depicting all species of wildfowl that he has photographed in the field. It is with this authoritative background that Richard Bishop brings to vivid life on canvas, and through etching, the majesty and exciting beauty of our wonderful world of wildfowl. All of his etchings and paintings depict birds in flight.

In this book you will find many, but certainly not all, of the answers to interesting questions about the major species of wildfowl in North America. And from this unique collection of wildfowl art by Richard Bishop you will surely derive many years of pleasure and inspiration.

Russ Williams

Contents

Contents *(Continued)*

COLOR REPRODUCTIONS

From *Prairie Wings* by Edgar M. Queeny

Dick Bishop sketching in a pin oak flat.

BLACK AND WHITE REPRODUCTIONS

THE MAGNIFICENT LEGACY

Let us imagine for a moment that we are able to turn back time while we stand on the vast rolling grasslands of the central plains as they were 150 years ago. As far as our eyes can see, the sweeping panorama of the prairie reaches to the far blue horizons. An ocean of distance and space. Its immensity is breathtaking. Rich, sun-drenched, and fertile. Buffalo country. Virgin range stretching unbroken to the foothills of the Rockies, and not an inch yet touched by the plow.

It is early April and the unmistakable signs of spring are everywhere. We can smell it in the gentle south wind, carrying the subtle fragrance of warming soil and greening grass, blended with the pungent tang of awakening marshes. The ice is but a few days gone from the potholes that dot this land.

But this is not what we came to see. This is only the stage and backdrop for the spectacular drama we are to witness, and even now is unfolding high overhead in the clear blue skies. The great exodus of waterfowl has begun. No words can possibly describe the wonder, the mystery and the awesome magnitude of this massive migration, as countless millions of ducks, geese, and swans leave their winter homes in the south for these prairies, the far northern tundra, Alaska and subarctic regions. These are their ancestral nesting grounds, and here they return to reproduce their kind in lush, bountiful, well-watered regions that provide their every need. Who can know how many centuries they have re-enacted this drama in an unchanging pattern along these same continental flyways?

As we wait in the early morning sun, the sky is filling with the dark, serpentine clouds of them, undulating and twisting as they form, break, and reform. On they come, wave after wave, flight after flight.

We know not what mystic power impels them or guides them on their way. And watching, we wonder at the nomadic yearning which grips and troubles the soul. Hour after hour their serried ranks keep pouring over the horizons. Far southward we see the distant strands approach like floating ribbons. Mallards, canvasbacks, pintails, Canada geese, snow geese, blue geese, whistling and trumpeter swans, and many other species of surface-feeding and diving waterfowl. At times, clouds of them darken the sun. By the thousands and millions, it seems, they march steadily through the heavens. The clamor of their constant calling and gabbling is sometimes deafening as they talk and back-talk, discussing the merits of resting waters below. Some break ranks, circle, and glide into the potholes and sloughs.

Yonder on the marsh they are packed so tightly we can see only a gleam of water here and there. The muddy shores are a solid blanket of ducks and geese of every variety, preening and basking in the sun. All through the day they throng through the sky, in a seemingly endless procession. Tomorrow, and for days, they will keep coming in living cataracts. The magnitude of this phenomenon staggers the imagination. It seems too unbelievable ever to have happened.

But this is the way it was — 150 years ago. All across the continent these enormous hordes moved northward, up the great Atlantic flyway, up the sprawling valleys of the Mississippi and Missouri, and the long Pacific coast. Abundance awaited them everywhere. Marshes, lakes, sloughs, rivers, and streams — clean and clear. Ample vegetation to fill their empty gizzards awaited at every rest stop, and lush grasses for every nesting need. No plows or sodbusters had yet defiled the land. No drainage of the wetlands had yet threatened their homes. And no armies of well-gunned hunters waited to slaughter them at every slough and pothole. This was waterfowl paradise.

And this was not all. Add now to these populous flocks of waterfowl more countless millions of other wildfowl — the quail, the wild turkey, grouse, prairie chicken, pigeons, doves, woodcock, partridge, and many more — all plentiful in vast numbers over the North American continent.

Yes, this is the way it was — 150 years ago. This was our magnificent legacy. The precious tokens of a land on which God and Nature had indeed smiled.

Shamefully, as a nation, we must confess that this priceless legacy has not always been well managed. The succeeding generations have wrought cataclysmic changes in the once beautiful, once bountiful land. Population, industry, science, land use, and public policy — all have borne heavily upon, and to the detriment of, the ducks, geese and wildfowl. We know well the importance of these changes man has made, but we do not seem to know their importance to wildfowl, or the importance of wildfowl to all of us.

A guilty conscience and a growing awareness of our trusteeship over our wildfowl and all wildlife have led us to spend millions of dollars to save what remains. The birds could very well live without us, but could we live without the birds?

It is very late, but perhaps not too late for an aroused public conscience to assure the perpetuation of this, our magnificent legacy.

Three Pintails

THE SURFACE-FEEDING DUCKS

THE SURFACE-FEEDING DUCKS, Subfamily Anatinae
   Mallard, Anas platyhrynchos platyhrynchos
   Mexican duck, Anas diazi novimexicana
   Black duck, Anas rubipres
   Mottled duck, Anas fulvigula maculosa
   Florida duck, Anas fulvigula fulvigula
   Gadwall, Anas strepera
   Pintail, Anas acuta
   Green-winged teal, Anas carolinensis
   Blue-winged teal, Anas discors discors
   Cinnamon teal, Anas cyanoptera septentrionalium
   American widgeon (baldpate), Mareca americana
   Shoveler, Spatula clypeata
   Wood duck, Aix sponsa

The thirty-five species of ducks common to North America can be conveniently grouped by habit or structure into major divisions or subfamilies. One of these subfamilies, the surface-feeding ducks — commonly called dabblers, puddlers, pond, and river ducks — prefer the shallow fresh water ponds, marshes, smaller streams, and inland lakes.

As the name suggests, this subfamily feeds on the water's surface, skimming up available vegetation along the shore, or tipping tail up and reaching down to the bottom to scoop up, in their broad, strainerlike bills, a great variety of submerged aquatic plant, animal, and insect life.

However, many ducks in this subfamily readily graze on land — and often do — especially in farmers' grain fields. They will even forage in deep woods for berries, nuts, and land insects. They have good locomotion on land, since their legs are set farther forward than most ducks.

In contrast to the subfamily of diving ducks, which prefer larger bodies of water and must make a long pattering run along the surface to take off, the puddle ducks fly almost vertically into flight for a quick getaway. To the human eye they appear to jump from the water. But the high-speed camera clearly demonstrates

(continued on page 25)

16

WORKING THE MARSH

Blue-Winged Teal, male *(Anas discors discors)*

17

SOLO FLIGHT

18

Wood Duck, male *(Aix sponsa)*

READY FOR SPLASHDOWN

Mallards *(Anas p. platyhrynchos)*

19

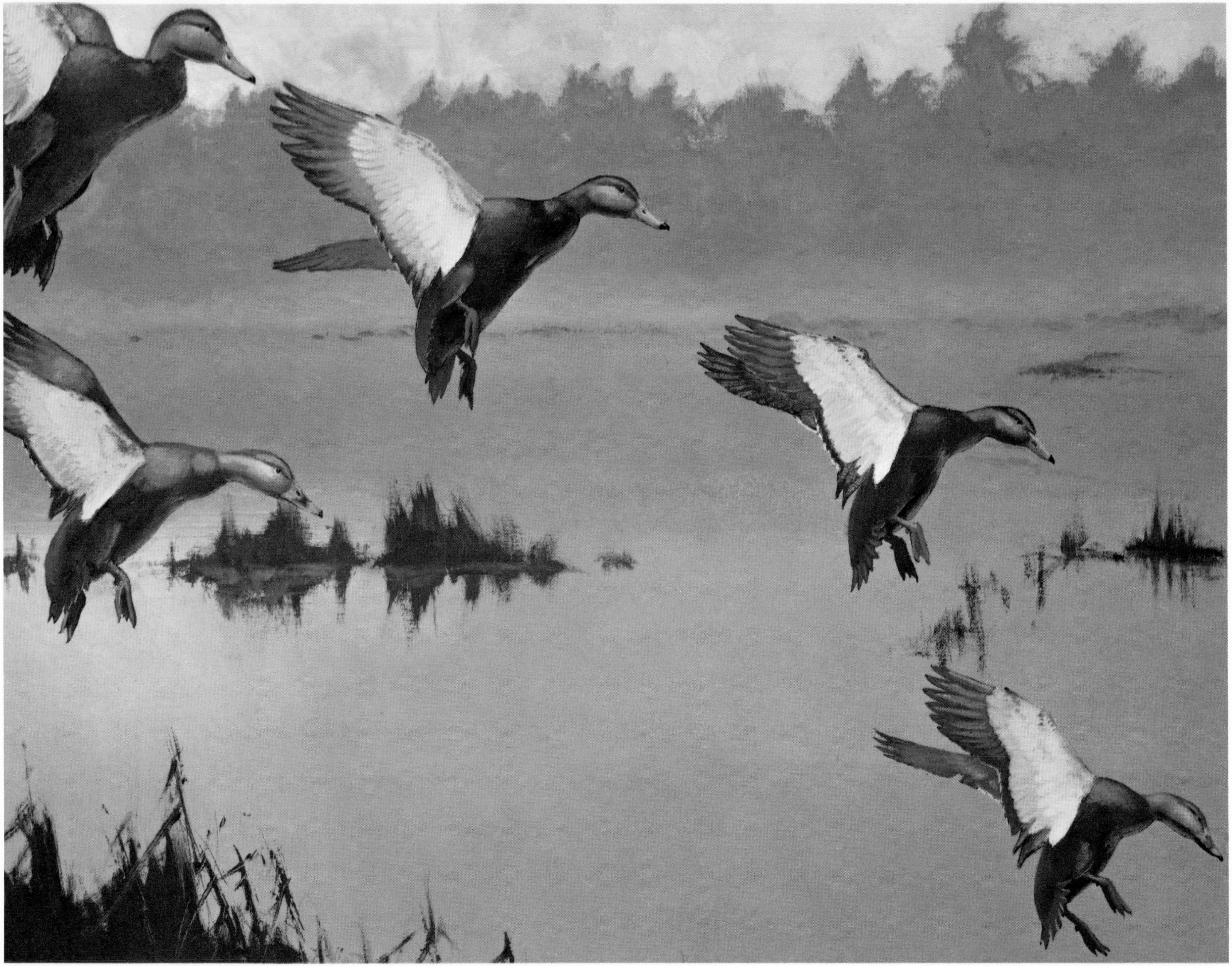

Reproduced by permission of Richard E. Bishop

LANDING FORMATION

Black Ducks *(Anas rubipres)*

GOING IT SINGLE

American Widgeon, baldpate, male *(Mareca americana)*

21

A LONELY PAIR

22

Pintails (*Anas acuta*)

FEEDING TIME

Shovelers *(Spatula clypeata)*

23

OUT OF THE CATTAILS

24

Green-Winged Teal, male *(Anas carolinensis)*

(continued from page 16)

that the wings are laid flat on the water, and with a mighty downbeat — so powerful that it bends the wings — the body is forced up and out of the water. With a rapid recovery stroke and paddling of webbed feet, the duck towers up and is off and away.

Aside from these generalizations, surface-feeding ducks are a diverse and far-ranging group, each species having its own peculiar traits and habits, but dabblers all.

The Mallard

In the quiet hush of a midsummer evening, I wander along the reedy shore of a small countryside pond. Suddenly, my solitude is shattered by a pair of startled ducks exploding from the nearby shallows. They hurtle up and over the trees, loudly quacking their resentment at the intrusion. I watch their retreating forms until they are swallowed up in the dusk. But I know they are mallards and will soon drift back to settle quietly here again. This little pond is their summer home, and somewhere in these rushes their ducklings are hiding, patiently waiting for their mother's reassuring call that all is well.

I think it is safe to say that the mallard is king of the ducks, at least from man's viewpoint. There are more mallards on all the flyways than any other species, and for thousands of years, the mallard has been of the greatest importance to man. It provided primitive man with food and through the centuries has continued to furnish him with more meat, eggs, and feathers than any of the ducks. It has long been the favorite of hunters everywhere. The mallard is universal in its distribution, inhabiting almost all of the northern hemisphere, and abounding in Europe, Asia, and Africa.

The mallard is a hardy and adaptable bird. It has survived tenaciously in great numbers, in spite of excessive shooting, inadequate protection, and dwindling water and nesting areas. While the mallard population today is still quite large, it is small compared to its fantastic abundance throughout North America fifty years ago. But because the mallard is a wary bird by nature and able to take care of himself when confronted with unusual conditions, he thrives amazingly well.

An adult mallard drake in full winter plumage is a handsome and colorful bird. His head and neck are a glistening, rich, iridescent green, tinged with a purplish gloss. His narrow white collar band, yellow bill, bright orange feet, chestnut breast, and colorful wings make the mallard drake one of the most distinctive and easily identified of all ducks. Mallards cross freely with other species of surface-feeding ducks, and since the offspring are usually fertile, it is common to see many hybrids among the various species.

The female is much more subdued in color. She is mottled brown and buff, similar to many of the other females in this subfamily. But what she lacks in color, she more than makes up for in noise. She is a mouthy one and does the talking for both. Her call is a resonant quack that has extraordinary carrying power. It is her raucous cry that hails passing flocks at great distances and brings them wheeling eagerly down to join the feeding. The drake, meanwhile, must be content to meekly listen and occasionally sound his soft, lisping, reedy quack that has little seductive appeal.

Usually the mallards lead off the migrating hordes as they vacate their winter homes in the southern states in February and March. They don't hurry and are content to move leisurely along in the footsteps of the retreating snow and ice, arriving in their breeding ranges in the northern prairies and marshes in late April and early May.

The wintering grounds for most mallards are in the lower half of the Mississippi valley, south of the frozen pond line. They loaf and feed through the winter months in the fresh water ponds, swamps, rice fields, streams, and everglades, growing fat on the abundant food in these havens. A few mallards will winter in the north if open water and feed are available. It is not unusual to see small mallard flocks in midwinter settled on a northern river or pond, kept partially open by springs or the warm discharge water of a nearby industrial plant or the moving of water by the birds themselves.

The prairie potholes, marshes, and small inland lakes of the northern states, central and western Canada, and Alaska, are the principal nesting grounds for mallards. They usually nest in the sloughs and marshes near the water, but nests may be found far from water on dry ground. Mallard nests have been found in the crotch of trees as high as twenty-five feet from the ground in heavily wooded areas, where the usual prairie site was nonexistent. Some say such nests are probably abandoned nests of hawks. Mallard nests are not fancy — just a hollow in the ground, lined with reeds and weeds, with some down from the female's breast.

A mallard hen with a brood of ducklings is a fiercely coura-

Overflow (Mallards)

geous mother, alert to every danger. As she leads her little ones to the water soon after hatching, she will give her note of alarm at the slightest hint of danger. The ducklings obediently scoot for cover under the rushes and grass, while the mother employs her repertoire of frantic tricks to divert the intruder's attention and lead him away from her precious babies. But despite her devotion, she will lose some to the many predators and will be fortunate to bring four or five safely through the summer.

Meanwhile, what about papa? Mallard drakes are no help to the brooding females. The drakes prefer to gather in small flocks and adjourn to the rushes, where they sulk and commiserate with each other as they wait out their eclipse moult, during which they also lose their flight feathers and are unable to fly until the new feathers grow in, usually by August.

All the mallards delight in sloshing about in the shallows of ponds, lakes, marshes, and sloughs, feeding on almost any vegetation or animal life available. They gobble up enormous quantities of pondweeds, duckweeds, sedges, smartweeds, wild celery, acorns, molluscs, insects, and dead fish. Studies have shown that they also consume enough mosquito pupae and larvae to be a real control factor in many areas.

When cool weather approaches, the mallards begin to assemble in flocks near their breeding grounds. As they grow more restless, their numbers build up rapidly into great throngs. They are ready for the long journey south, yet reluctant to leave as long as feed and open water are available. The mallards that furnish hunters the early season shooting are usually the locals and more southern-bred birds. These mallards are neither as large nor as colorful as the far-northern mallards that the hunters eagerly await late in the season.

Then, overnight, the season's first serious cold snap strikes, and a cap of ice seals the ponds and lakes. Now they know the time has come, and the grand passage southward begins, in what is surely one of nature's most spectacular events.

The Black Duck

It is always a rewarding experience to sit quietly along shore and observe black ducks as they descend to the pond. What a beautiful picture they make as their smooth bodies, with curved wings rigidly set, come gliding in, tilting slightly from side to side. They circle just enough to check momentum, lower their big red feet like landing gear, and with a few quick flaps, drop down and ski gently into the water with a soft splash.

Along the Atlantic flyway, the big, splendid black duck, larger than most, is the dominant bird, both in numbers and preference by hunters. A quarter of a million black ducks are taken annually by hunters, authorities say. But in spite of this toll, the black seems to thrive and remain fairly plentiful.

The black duck is like the mallard in many of its habits. It resembles the female mallard in appearance, although larger. Many hunters call it "black mallard" and it associates frequently with migrating mallards. However, its range is confined largely to the eastern and central portions of North America, and particularly along the Atlantic seaboard.

Black Ducks scouting around

A lonely Black Duck (Redleg)

The black is extremely shy — the most cautious and wary of all our ducks. It is a swift and powerful flier. Its keen eye and persistent distrust of man and his decoys make the black duck the supreme test for hunters who consider its meat the equal of the mallard.

They dabble and feed in ponds, sloughs, and shallow water much the same as the mallards. But along the eastern coast, they feed on considerably more animal food than does the mallard.

Although the black is a large, graceful, and handsome duck, it lacks the brilliant plumage of the mallard drake. Both sexes are alike in appearance. As its name implies, it is a dark, dusky, sooty, mottled brown, similar to, but darker than, the female mallard. The absence of the two white bars bordering the purple speculum on the wings distinguishes the black from the female mallard. On the black duck, only one narrow white bar borders the back edge of the speculum.

The black duck is a skilled and conscientious nest builder. Its nests are usually well hidden and seldom seen by human beings. It builds in all sorts of situations in both fresh water and salt marshes, on stumps over the water, tree cavities, underbrush, edges of swamps and woods, and on dry ground. Nesting areas range from North Carolina north to the tree line in eastern Canada, and westward into Ontario and the Great Lakes.

They filter southward along the Atlantic flyway in September, but the migration peak comes in early November. They seem to prefer staying as far north as open water and weather permit. During the winter, most blacks congregate in the tidal areas and fresh water swamps and marshes from New Jersey to South Carolina.

Black ducks have been divided into two subspecies. The red-legged black duck is identified by its coral-red feet, yellow bill, heavier feathering, and larger size. It is presumed to be the more northern-bred of the two, and a later migrant. The common black duck, designated as the smaller, has brownish feet and a green bill. It is considered the more southerly breeder and an earlier migrant. Many ornithologists, however, do not agree that the black should be divided into two varieties. The American Ornithologists' Union no longer recognizes the separation of the black duck into two subspecies.

The Pintail

There they are, high overhead! Pintails! Their sleek white forms flash in the sun. Suddenly, in perfect unison, they bank sharply and come volplaning down, with reckless abandon, straight for the water. Down, down they come with incredible speed. I hold my breath in awe as I watch their spectacular dive. Just as it seems they will surely crash, they pull up and with the precision of a well-drilled fighter squadron swoop over me in a

mighty swish. And without a single wing stroke, they glide on down the bay, just skimming the water's surface. What thrilling fliers these pintails are!

When the first faint hint of spring is in the air and the ice is still firm on the northern lakes, you may see flying high overhead the swift-moving flocks of slender-bodied, long-necked ducks with pointed tails. These are the hardy pintails, the advance troops, pushing impatiently northward to their nesting ranges in the subarctic areas of Alaska, western and central Canada, and the prairies of the northern states. In the still-wintry north they may find no resting place, and storms and bitter cold may turn them back for a time, but undaunted, they keep coming.

The pintail is remarkably handsome—almost elegant, in fact. Its slender form, long-pointed wings, elongated tail, and long, swanlike neck give it a dashing and streamlined figure. In the air and on the water, the pintail is probably the most graceful of all ducks. They are swift, powerful, and agile fliers—exciting to watch as they come swooping down from on high and over the water with the speed of an arrow, in an awesome display of aerial finesse. Flocks of pintails have been timed by airplane pilots at sixty-five miles an hour. Hunters say pintails can do ninety for short stretches. Some pintails migrate across the two thousand miles of Pacific Ocean from their breeding grounds in Alaska to the Hawaiian Islands.

Pintails have a variety of colloquial names—gray duck, smee, sprig, pinnie, and many others that are in local use wherever the pintail ranges.

The breeding range of the pintail is the most far-reaching of all ducks, and like the mallard, it is one of the best known and most easily recognized species of North American wildfowl. It is cherished by hunters, both as a challenging target and duck dinner. Pintails are prolific when conditions are right, but decidedly desultory when they are wrong. Their numbers fluctuate accordingly.

In spite of his elegance, poise, and speed, the pintail is very shy, ever on the alert for danger. Only the inexperienced hunter underestimates the pintail and his keen eye. He is also a quiet bird, not given to much noisy chatter or calling, like some of his cousins in this subfamily. Pintails rarely call, either in flight or on the water. The male sounds a mellow whistle, while the female has a quack similar to that of the mallard hen.

The nest of a pintail hen is usually a deep hollow scooped out of the ground, with vegetation and down for a lining. She prefers low but dry ground, often at some distance from water. She

Pintails in a rice field

will lay an average of ten eggs, pale olive green, resembling mallard eggs. She tends the nest alone for twenty-three days, although the drake may stand by until he begins to moult. He then slips off, to hide out until his full plumage returns. Many stories are told of the remarkable courage of pintails in defense of their young, and their demonstrations of parental solicitude are quite touching.

Like the other members of the surface-feeding subfamily, pintails are dabblers and like to feed in the shallows, tipping up, tails in the air, to explore the bottoms for weed seeds, plants, and vege-

33

tation of all kinds. Its diet is 90 percent vegetable and its feeding habits are much the same as the mallard. Usually the pintail will not feed as much on dry land as the mallard does.

One odd thing about the pintails. Although they are eager beavers to hurry north in the early spring, when the north country offers such uninviting accommodations, they are among the first to high-tail it south at the first suggestion of the approaching cold of winter. Pintails are in the vanguard of the first ducks sweeping down the great flyways, along with the tender little blue-winged teal. In the Mississippi flyway, they may start south in late August or early September. But in the warmer flyway regions, the peak flight of pintails is usually much later.

The pintail is truly one of our most prized waterfowl—a joy to watch and admire, on the water and in the air. He is a smart fellow—so smart that it could be, if the struggle for survival goes too hard against our waterfowl, the pintail, along with his cautious cousin, the black duck, may outlast all the others.

The Baldpate

Out over the marsh we can see a flock of ducks in tight formation, whipping and wheeling about like pigeons around a barn. Now they zig-zag our way, then seeing us, flare up and over, the drakes sounding their whistlelike alarm. Baldpates! The nervous nellies of duckdom. And also known as the American widgeon, close relative of the European widgeon.

Very interesting birds, these baldpates. Nonconformists that refuse to follow the usual behavioral patterns of a duck. They steal from their neighbors. They would rather loaf during daylight and eat at night, when respectable ducks prefer to sleep. They dote on lettuce and spinach in the truck gardeners' fields.

These devilish little dabblers are pesty nuisances for the diving ducks, especially canvasbacks and redheads. The baldpate rides herd on the deep-water ducks, and when these diligent divers come up from the bottom with a bill full of wild celery or other choice morsels, the baldpate is right there to snatch it away before the diver can swallow his tidbit. Why the diving ducks tolerate being robbed of the fruit of their honest labors is one of the mysteries that remain unsolved by ornithologists.

Anything goes with the baldpate in order to satisfy his gourmet appetite. In the Imperial Valley of California the baldies en-

34

Baldpates deep in the marsh

35

joy dropping in, uninvited, on the valley's lush lettuce and spinach fields for free lunch at the farmers' expense.

Although he is a shameless rascal, the baldpate is innocently good-looking, colorful, and very graceful. On the water, he sits primly and lightly. On land, he scampers about like a young chicken, grazing on green grass and other vegetation. In the air, baldpates fly with abandon — swiftly and in small, compact flocks. They are jittery and spook easily, flying straight up off the water with a great clattering of wings and then twisting off. The male has a wild and musical voice that resembles a piping whistle. The female merely utters a ducklike qua-awk.

Another odd thing about these baldpates — they are real fraidy-cats, but they are also very curious. They're so curious that, in spite of their shy, wild disposition, they will return again and again over hunters' decoys.

Baldpates are rather indifferent nest builders. They build on dry ground, sometimes far from the water, and with no attempt at concealment. Since they arrive late in the spring, they are late nesters. When they are not pestering the diving ducks, baldpates like to puddle around, in the manner of all surface-feeding ducks in this subfamily, and will feed during the day unless disturbed. But if they have an uneasiness about their safety or feel insecure, they will hide and sulk in the rushes, coming out to feed only after dark.

In early autumn — usually September — the baldpates start south from their nesting grounds in all parts of the prairies and the far north in Canada and Alaska. They winter along the Atlantic and Pacific coasts, the Gulf, Mexico, and Central America.

The Gadwall

It seems rather strange that the gadwall duck should have nearly world-wide distribution and yet be relatively unknown to so many hunters. In some regions it is abundant, in others almost entirely absent.

The gadwall is smaller than a mallard but resembles it in general appearance at a distance and is sometimes mistaken for a mallard hen or baldpate hen. It is much lighter in color than the mallard hen — almost gray — and is called "gray duck" by many hunters. Gadwalls are the only surface-feeding ducks with a white speculum, but even with this distinctive wing mark, the gadwall is difficult for most observers to identify.

One bit of upmanship that the gadwall has over his surface-feeding cousins is his ability to dive in fairly deep water for his food, if necessary. However, like the other dabblers, the gadwall would rather just dabble and splash around in shallow water, tipping tail up to reach down and explore the bottom for whatever is available. It likes to break away from the water and go wandering around on land, visiting grain fields and even the woods when it can find acorns and nuts.

Gadwalls, unlike most of the puddle ducks, don't go much for the far north country as a place to nest. They confine themselves to the prairie states and southern provinces of Canada and seldom go as far north as mallards and pintails. The open prairie country is their domain, and here they build well concealed nests in the dry grasses, usually away from the water. But gadwalls also have a liking for nesting on islands in the larger lakes. The dwindling prairie lands and encroachment of agriculture has not helped the gadwall, and this may account for its irregular distribution in North America.

Gadwalls fly very swiftly but do not engage in the fancy acrobatics and stunting of the pintails and baldpates. They are strictly straight arrow and fly the shortest line to wherever they're going. They will frequently associate with baldpates and pintails, however, and when they are with baldpates it is easy to pick them out of the flock on the water. The baldpate rests very lightly on the surface and seems to sit high. The gadwall is just the opposite. He sits low and flat.

Compared to the hardy go-go mallard, the gadwall is a softy when it comes to leaving its warm winter home to go north. It hangs back until all the ice is out of the ponds before it ventures north. When their nesting is completed, and the youngsters are barely able to fly, every gadwall lights out for the south, the earlier the better.

The Shoveler

We were paddling slowly through the swamp early one summer morning, just enjoying the eerie silence, when we heard a disturbance in the water around a little point of rushes. As we eased the canoe ahead, we saw three ducks so engrossed in their feeding they failed to notice us. They seemed to be perform-

Spoonies (Shovelers) coming in

ing some strange ritual. They swam rapidly in little circles, one behind the other, with chattering bills submerged in the water and making quite a racket. I never saw such enthusiastic feeding, but I recognized the ducks and remembered this was the way these colorful little dabblers sometimes went about their feeding. They were shovelers, more commonly called spoonbills, or spoonies, and an assortment of other names.

No other duck has a bill like the shoveler's. It is doubtful if other ducks would want it. It is broad, flat, disproportionately large, longer than the head, and gives the bird a rakish, top-heavy, ungraceful appearance. With this highly specialized snorkel, the shoveler is the most proficient of all the surface-feeding ducks when it's time to put on the feed bag. The comblike teeth in the bill are more highly developed than in other ducks. By submerging this scoop shovel in the water and swimming along rapidly, the shoveler can slurp up large quantities of tiny food particles, taste them with its sensitive tongue, and sift out unwanted bits through the teeth. Sort of a continuous mass production system. Sometimes the shoveler likes to rummage around down on the bottom in the muck and slush the mud through its bill, retaining what is edible and rejecting the remainder. When several shovelers feed together, they may use the ring-around-the-rosy procedure described above. The idea apparently is for the duck ahead to stir up the water for the one following, making more of the tiny food particles available.

The shoveler is a gay dresser. On the water, he shows more white than any other surface-feeder. This and his oversized, sloping bill make him easy to identify on the water. But on the wing, it's not so easy. He is often mistaken for a mallard and resembles blue-winged teal in structure. He is quite small—smaller than the mallard, but larger than teal.

Shovelers are not impressive fliers—usually rather slow, although their wing beat is faster and noisier than that of the mallard. But they are strong fliers, and one of the few that wing it nonstop from Alaska to Hawaii. They are not as wary as they should be, and make easy marks for hunters. Many times hunters will see shovelers circle and return to decoys after being shot at.

But for all its big mouth, the shoveler has little to say. Its voice is rather weak and about all it can manage is a low gutteral call, both male and female.

Distribution is wide, throughout North America, Europe, and Asia. Nesting range in North America is confined to the uplands of the northern states, the prairies and marshes of western Canada, and up into central Alaska. It nests on the ground in dry grass and weeds.

Another odd feature about the shoveler is the tendency of the female to prefer two husbands during the mating and nesting season. After the two adults have paired, a second male may show up and join the family. He is usually a young drake in moult who finds the young females have gone off by themselves and are not ready to pair until next season.

Like the little blue-winged teal, shovelers are fair-weather fowl and detest cold weather. They check out, bag and baggage, and flee south in early autumn, often flying with the teal. They winter in the southern states and Mexico. In the spring, they seldom start north until the ponds and potholes are completely clear of ice.

The Green-Winged Teal

One fall afternoon when I was a lad of thirteen, I took my dad's old 12-gauge pump gun and walked along the small creek that wound through our farm pasture. Maybe I could jump some ducks. Sure enough, at the first bend a pair of teal clattered up. Somehow I got off two quick shots, and to my utter amazement both birds dropped on the grass across the creek. It had to be beginner's luck. Only the experts shoot teal doubles. I waded over and picked up one. It was a pretty little female green-wing. She was so small and delicate, I felt a twinge of remorse as I held the limp, warm body in my hand. Such a tender little creature to kill. I was sure the other was the male, but after searching the grass I failed to find it. I was about to give up when I spied him, neatly curled up, stone dead, in the deep imprint of a cow track in the soft mud. Apparently, he had plumped straight into the hole, and the impact rolled him up like a ball. It was a proud moment showing off a teal double at home, but somehow I never again had a desire to shoot at teal. I always remembered that lovely little green-wing lying lifeless in my hand.

If there were beauty pageants for ducks, the dapper little green-winged teal would be a top-ranking contender. And if there were duck races he would probably be an easy winner, although he is the smallest of our ducks. The greenie is a beautiful and dynamic little fireball.

Green-winged teal are abundant in all the major flyways during migration, but their nesting grounds are centered in the vast prai-

(continued on page 49)

FLIGHT PATTERN

Canvasback Ducks (*Aythya valisineria*)

41

OUT OF THE STORM

Canvasback Ducks *(Aythya valisineria)*

WHISTLING IN

Common Goldeneye Ducks *(Bucephala clangula americana)*

43

OVER THE MARSH

Ring-Necked Ducks (*Aythya collaris*)

READY FOR LANDING

Greater Scaup Ducks (*Aythya marila neartica*)

45

DAWN PATROL

Greater Scaup Ducks (*Aythya marila neartica*)

CEILING ZERO

Redhead Ducks (*Aythya americana*)

47

SKYWARD BOUND

48

Redhead Duck, male *(Aythya americana)*

(continued from page 40)

rie regions of the northern states and western Canada. They love the sloughs, potholes, and streams of the inland country, and here they build pretty little nests, well constructed, and concealed in long grass.

When the young families are ready to fly, and the first touch of cool weather signals autumn's approach, the greenies pick up and head south. But they dawdle and linger along the way as long as the weather is good and feed plentiful.

If you want to see some great stunt flying, go out and watch the green-wings. They seem to enjoy high-balling along at incredible speeds in tightly packed formations. You'll see them roll and twist in daredevil turns with perfect precision, wing-tip to wing-tip, as though controlled by some mechanical signal. Some ornithologists claim green-winged teal can hit 100 miles an hour or more. Many hunters who have swung a gun too late at a flock of passing greenies would say that's a gross understatement.

The Blue-Winged Teal

Nearly every pothole, slough, and marshy lake in the northern prairie regions shelters a pair or more of nesting blue-winged teal during the warm summer months. And here these dainty little dabblers return year after year, seldom visiting the seacoasts. The teal thrives, or seems to hold its own at least, in spite of continued drainage of wetlands, the encroachment of industry and agriculture, and the heavy toll taken by hunters both in the United States and Mexico, where it winters.

The blue-wings are reluctant to leave their warm winter homes until really hot weather prevails on the northern prairies. They are therefore very late nesters. But the young develop rapidly and are usually ready to fly by August. As soon as the youngsters are awing, the teal begin to gather in nervous little flocks and prepare to hit the long and hazardous trail south. When the first touch of frost comes to the lowlands in August, the teal vanish overnight and begin to pour down the Central and Mississippi flyways, where the opening day hunters are waiting. The early season bags usually contain many teal, both locals and the earlier migrants.

The blue-wings are speed demons, like the green-wings, and they can swish over a set of decoys like a squadron of jet bombers and be far down the marsh before the hunter can raise his gun. But the teal fly in close formation and, in spite of their swiftness,

are relatively easy targets for the skilled hunters.

Unlike the other dabbling ducks, the blue-wings prefer not to tip up when feeding, with feet and tail out of the water. They seem satisfied to work in the more shallow water and eat whatever can be handily reached. They especially like wild rice, but consume a variety of soft aquatic vegetation, and some animal matter.

The nest of the blue-wing is neat and basketlike, on the ground and usually close to water. The female is a good mother and keeps her nest well secreted from prowlers and predators. Each time she returns to the nest, she will alight at some distance and slip quietly through the grass to the nest, rather than betray the nesting site.

On the water, blue-winged teal can be identified by the bright blue wing patch of both sexes. The male voice is a whistling peep, usually repeated rapidly. The female has a faint quack, of much less volume than the female green-wing.

The Cinnamon Teal

For some unexplained reason, the cinnamon teal is an all-westerner, and will have it no other way. He just loves the west, and who can quarrel with his judgment? He prefers the shallow tule-bordered lakes and marshes of the far western states and has no inclination to leave. So the cinnamon is the only North American duck with both wintering and breeding range confined strictly to the west, and concentrated west of the Rocky Mountains. The cinnamon is rarely found east of this divide. Oddly enough, another population of the cinnamon is found two thousand miles away in southern South America, but the two are never joined in migration.

Cinnamon and blue-winged teal are much alike. The cinnamon is a bit larger than the blue-wing and has a longer, heavier bill. Both cinnamon and blue-wing females are very similar, separated only by the slight differences in bills, and some minor color variations. The male cinnamon is a rich, dark cinnamon red on body and neck, and is easily identified among the teal.

The breeding and wintering ranges of the cinnamon overlap, thus making the migration a rather casual movement a bit farther south, more of a shift than a flight. The nests are well made, like the blue-wing's nest. The male—and this is very unusual for ducks—does not desert the nesting female. He seems much more willing than other male ducks to share some responsibility as a parent. He hangs around during incubation and when the ducklings hatch, assumes the role of protector, and will put up an impressive fight against predators. The cinnamon duckling is more adept at escape from danger than other ducklings. Ornithologists have reported seeing frightened ducklings dive and swim great distances under water until they reach shore, where they hide under moss or grass.

Like the blue-wings and green-wings, the cinnamon teal are swifties on the wing. Their flight style is much the same as the blue-wing, and hunters find them an elusive target. But they are popular game with the western hunters and just as delicious eating as the other teal.

Ducks of Limited Range

The New Mexican duck is, in a manner of speaking, a mallard that is so fond of the Rio Grande river valley, it just stays there the year around. It resembles the mallard in general habits, and both sexes of the New Mexican duck are similar in appearance to the female mallard. It makes its permanent home in the Rio Grande valley from El Paso, Texas, to Albuquerque, New Mexico, and does not migrate. The New Mexican duck will mingle with mallards that happen along, but will not be lured away to other regions. It is considered by observers to be a stronger and faster flyer than the mallard, and extremely wary.

*

The Florida duck is almost identical in general coloration of body plumage to the black duck, and the two are closely related. Their habits are similar and there seems to be little to distinguish between them, except that the Florida duck restricts its range to southern and central portions of Florida, does not migrate, and is not of great importance to the hunters.

*

The mottled duck in all its habits and general appearance is very similar to its near relative and neighbor, the Florida duck. It is also a close relative of the black duck which it resembles. The range of the mottled duck is restricted to Louisiana and Texas, where it remains throughout the year, refusing to migrate with other waterfowl.

The Wood Duck

The wood duck is a creature of such exotic plumage and unducklike behavior that it hardly seems like a duck at all. There are many handsome ducks, but woodie is the grandest and gaudiest of all. He doesn't quack like a duck; he squeals, whistles, and peeps. He doesn't nest on the ground or in the rushes like a duck; he nests in a hole in a tree like a woodpecker, or in man-made houses like a bluebird. And he perches on tree limbs like a chicken. He is, nevertheless, a duck, and a fully accredited member of the subfamily of surface-feeding ducks.

Woodie likes to play the role of escapist and get away from it all back in the woods. He loves the secluded, wooded bottomlands and impenetrable swamps, yet he has been seen nesting in towns. Wood ducks are found almost everywhere in the eastern half of the United States, and to a very limited extent in the Pacific Northwest and British Columbia. Actually, the bulk of them breeds in the eastern one-third of the continent. In 1962, banding and kill data indicated a population of four hundred thousand pairs of wood ducks. But they are not as plentiful as they could be, or should be. The habitat of the wood duck has suffered seriously from civilization. Drainage, lumbering, and urbanization have eliminated more than half of its natural breeding habitat.

Wood ducks are a choice bird for hunters, and one of the most important in the Atlantic flyway. Some years ago, wood ducks were near extinction from constant persecution by overhunting and by feather hunters who collected the skins for making artificial trout and salmon flies. But we finally woke up and enacted protective legislation, just in time to keep woodie from going the way of the passenger pigeon. Many states closed the wood duck season; other states permit only one or two in a bag limit.

When woodie has his druthers about nesting sites, he prefers an abandoned woodpecker hole in a hollow tree. It may be deep in the woods, beside a pond or lake, or in a remote swamp. The hole may be as high as forty or fifty feet above ground. If no hollow tree is available, he has a way of improvising. Wood ducks have been seen nesting on hay stacks and even inside barns. In recent years, more and more people have been coming to woodie's rescue by erecting nesting houses in suitable locations. The wood ducks readily take to these houses and return to them year after year.

The question of the young leaving the nest high up in a tree always comes up. The truth is, the downy young wood ducks

A true North American native
(The Wood Duck)
From *Prairie Wings* by Edgar M. Queeny

simply jump out at the mother's bidding and plummet down to the ground, bounce a bit, get up, wiggle their little tails a time or two and are ready for a swim. Apparently, they were made for bailing out of trees, and are none the worse for it. The idea that the mother carries them down has been pretty well discredited by motion pictures of the ducklings taking the big plunge into space.

Wood ducks dabble and eat in the shallow water much the same as all the other surface-feeders. They consume lots of vegetation, about the same varieties as other ducks. The wood duck is a swift and nimble flyer with an uncanny skill for darting and twisting through the trees and heavy woods. It seems odd to see them at times perched in chummy flocks high up in the trees, like flocks of roosting chickens. But their favorite perch is a fallen log near the water, where they like to relax and preen.

Since they do not breed farther north than the southern edge of Canada, wood ducks have a relatively short migration journey to the inland waters of the southern states for the winter. They depart at the beginning of autumn, and return north quite early, just as the ice leaves their ponds and timbered swamps.

The Tree Ducks

The black-bellied tree duck, *Dendrocygna autumnalis fulgens,* is common in Mexico, visits in Texas quite regularly, and other southern states occasionally. This rather odd-looking bird appears as though it could be a cross between a duck and a goose, and really seems to be more goose than duck, with its very long, gooselike legs and neck. It perches in trees, and in Mexico is a bit of a pest when it descends on corn fields to feed. Black-bellied ducks do nest in forks of tree branches and in tree holes, but they will also nest on the ground among the rushes and grass. There is no noticeable migration.

*

The fulvous tree duck, *Dendrocygna bicolor helva,* frequents southwestern parts of the United States, from Texas to southern California, as well as northern Mexico. The fulvous tree duck closely resembles the black-bellied tree duck, and both species are vegetarians, grazing like geese and tipping up to feed in shallow water like pond ducks. They often feed at night and spend their days in the reeds and along shores of ponds and lagoons. The name "tree duck" is somewhat of a misnomer for the fulvous because it is neither a tree percher nor much of a tree nester. It will sometimes nest in hollow tree holes, but usually the nests are in the tules or grass along the edges of ponds and swamps. It has a surprising range in widely separated colonies, found in India, southeastern South America, northern Mexico, East Africa, southern United States, and northern South America.

BLACK-BELLIED TREE DUCKS
By Bob Hines—U.S. Dept. of Interior, Fish and Wildlife Service

THE DIVING DUCKS

THE DIVING DUCKS, Subfamily Aythyinae
  Redhead, Aythya americana
  Ring-necked duck, Aythya collaris
  Canvasback, Aythya valisineria
  Greater scaup, Aythya marila neartica
  Lesser scaup, Aythya affinis
  American or Common goldeneye, Bucephala clangula americana
  Barrow's goldeneye, Bucephala islandica
  Bufflehead, Bucephala albeola
  Old Sqaw, Clangula hyemalis
  Harlequin duck, Histrionicus histrionicus
  Steller's eider, Polysticta stelleri
  Common eider, Somateria mollissima borealis
              Somateria mollissima dresseri
              Somateria mollissima sedentaria
              Somateria mollissima v. nigra
  King eider, Somateria spectabilis
  Spectacled eider, Lampronetta fischeri
  White-winged scoter, Melanitta deglandi deglandi
              Melanitta deglandi dixoni
  Surf scoter, Melanitta perspicillata
  American scoter, Oidemia nigra americana

The subfamily of diving ducks is the second important group having characteristics that definitely separate it from the subfamily of surface-feeding ducks. The divers are also called sea ducks or bay ducks, but we will adopt the more popular name, diving ducks, for our use here.

The diving ducks, in contrast to surface-feeders, prefer the open water, deeper water, the large inland lakes and bays where they can dive for their food, often to considerable depths. Thus they are not commonly seen in many of the grass-covered lakes, small ponds, and sloughs that attract the surface-feeding ducks. However, some diving ducks nest in the same prairie regions and large marsh areas where the surface-feeders nest. A number of the diving ducks are seagoing and live most of their lives on the oceans and salt water.

The food of diving ducks differs from the surface-feeders. Divers subsist on less vegetable matter than the surface-feeders, and more on molluscs, shellfish, and other aquatic animal matter. They are strong, efficient divers, but far less mobile on land than the surface-feeders. Their legs are set farther back on the body, and while this increases their swimming and diving capabilities, it renders them very awkward on solid ground, and accounts for their pronounced waddle.

A distinctive characteristic of diving ducks is their manner of rising from the water to fly. Unlike the surface-feeders, which fly straight up out of the water in a quick power stroke, the divers must make a long pattering run for it, flapping their wings and kicking their feet on the water until they gain enough speed to be airborne, much the same as aircraft. This need for a long runway is another reason the diving ducks do not use small ponds.

As a group, the diving ducks are not as brilliantly colored as the surface-feeders. And with a few exceptions — celery-fed canvasbacks, for example — the flesh of diving ducks is not as tasty as that of the surface-feeders, due to their dietary habits.

The Redhead Duck

I was about twelve when my dad took me on my first real duck hunting trip in the Iowa bottomlands along the Missouri River. It was still dark when he put me in a small blind by myself, while he occupied another blind a short distance down the lake. The decoys had been set out the night before. It was bitter cold, and I dozed off while waiting for the dawn. Suddenly something snapped me awake. By now it was nearly daylight, and I was astonished to see the water around the decoys alive with real ducks. Mallards? No, redheads! A flock of big fat redheads had sneaked into the decoys while I snoozed. I swung the gun to my shoulder and bedlam broke loose as the air was filled with the flailing wings of terror-stricken ducks. I fired, blindly I'm sure, into the most concentrated part of the confusion. Then fired again. But not a single duck fell. And in a moment they were gone. As I watched these redheads high-tail it down the lake, I wondered if dad had been watching. And for a moment I wished I were home in my warm bed.

This was my first encounter with the popular redhead duck, one of the prominent members of the subfamily of divers. We don't see the redhead as frequently or in as great numbers as we did some years ago, mostly because much of its preferred habitat, the prairie marsh, has gone down the drain. In recent years, hunting restrictions on redheads have been very severe. They are delicious eating, and hunters prize them highly.

The redhead is a big duck, a bit smaller than its cousin, the canvasback, for which it is often mistaken. The male redhead has a dark maroon head and neck, black breast, and gray body. When you see the canvasback and redhead together on the water, their differences are quite evident. The redhead has a round head with a high forehead and a small, short bill. The canvasback's head is long, with a sloping forehead and a long sloping bill, almost as long as its head. Both ducks will mingle and feed together, and in many ways have similar habits.

Redheads apparently are not as intelligent as some ducks. They do some pretty stupid things that don't help perpetuate their species. They often decoy with ridiculous ease, and will just barrel in and plunk down among the wooden blocks without the slightest hesitation or reconnoitering. And then, after the flock absorbs a

They are returning (Redheads)

fusillade of shot, they will swing around and come right back for more. Or they will circle down the lake and repeat the performance at another hunter's blind. On the other hand, the redhead can be exasperatingly smart. Like rafting up by the hundreds out in the middle of a large lake or bay, well out of gun range of frustrated hunters. And there they'll sit all day, happily diving, feeding, and voicing that peculiar call that sounds like a tomcat.

The redhead is not a fancy flyer. He just flies straight and steady. In migration, redheads travel fast and usually in the traditional V-formation more frequently than other ducks. They do have one interesting habit that may indicate some degree of intelligence after all. They take a morning and evening constitutional. In the morning and again in the evening, great rafts of them rise off the water like a blanket, fly high up, and go sailing around and around, up and down the lake or bay. Then they return and settle down again and raft up in the deep water.

These ducks, like all the divers, are essentially deep-water addicts and prefer the big, open waters. They do not go far north to nest, refusing to desert the prairie marshes of the northern central states and central Canada. They like to nest in the rushes over the water, sometimes quite far from shore. They are not particularly devoted to parenthood, and will often dispose of their offspring by laying their eggs in the nests of other species, especially the unsuspecting canvasback. No other duck is so wasteful of its eggs or such a nuisance to the other ducks which nest in the same

REDHEAD AND BROOD
By Bob Hines—U.S. Dept. of Interior, Fish and Wildlife Service

marshes. They migrate south in October usually, not far behind the canvasbacks. They return north about the middle of March after wintering along the west coast, the Gulf, and Mexico, with a few along the Atlantic coast.

The Ring-Necked Duck

The once-plentiful ring-necked duck is no longer as abundant on any of the major flyways during fall migration as it was years ago. The ringnecks at one time furnished good hunting in most of the flyways. In the Mississippi flyway it is still probably more numerous than any of the other divers during fall migration. Ringnecks are vulnerable targets, however, because they frequent areas easily accessible to hunters. And since they are not as wary as they should be, and decoy easily, they suffer heavy losses during hunting seasons. Most hunters consider the ringneck good eating and preferable to the scaups.

Ringnecks are small and resemble the lesser scaup (bluebill) in both habits and appearance. This similarity causes some confusion among the hunters. Many hunters call it "marsh bluebill" because it nests and feeds in the marshes of the prairie country and for its summer range seems to prefer the smaller waters, although it is a diver. Ringnecks are ornithologically more closely related to the redhead than to the lesser scaup that it resembles.

Like the scaup, ringnecks move north early in the spring, even before the ice has gone from the lakes. And in the fall they may hang around until all the ponds and marshes are frozen over solid. Hunters will see many of them sitting and sliding about on the ice around the last small hole on the lake to freeze over, as though reluctant to leave for the south.

On the wing they move in small groups, rarely in large flocks. Unlike many ducks, they will descend to the water in a straight, direct line without the customary circling maneuver.

The nest of ringnecks is well concealed among the reeds, rushes, cattails, and long grass in wet, boggy places, sometimes almost at water level.

The ringneck is an expert diver and has been known to go down forty feet for its food. It eats about the same diet as other fresh water divers — mostly vegetation and some aquatic animal matter. It is such a strong, swift diver that it can easily catch minnows and frogs.

The summer breeding range is confined quite definitely to the north central states and south central Canada. The Gulf states, south Atlantic states, parts of Mexico, and northern South America are its principal wintering grounds.

The Canvasback

Here is the glamor bird of the flyways. Big, heavy-bodied, powerful, and handsome. The epicure's delight. That's the canvasback. If the mallard has a challenger for his kingly status among hunters, it has to be the lordly canvasback—often called "whiteback."

Years ago the canvasbacks swarmed down the flyways in mighty hordes in their late fall migration. But no more do they swarm in hordes. So much of their original nesting range has been destroyed, their population has declined drastically over the years. The cans, it seems, have been up-and-downers for many years. Some years they seem almost plentiful, then they dwindle, varying with weather and drought conditions in the breeding ranges.

The canvasbacks are exciting birds. It is a pleasant and rewarding experience just to watch them. They fly at tremendous speeds, and there is some disagreement about whether the canvasback or the green-winged teal is the faster flyer. It would be interesting to have them race and settle the issue.

The cans are exceedingly hardy and this encourages many to loiter in the north country very late in the fall. They seem to cherish their northern summer homes so much, they dislike to leave early with other ducks. Most have left by mid-October, but some always hang back until bruising weather forces them out, and when they finally come roaring down the flyways, riding a bitter gale or snowstorm, they are exciting to behold.

I recall sitting on a hill in western Minnesota late one October afternoon when a nasty snowstorm was beginning to blow in. It was cold and the howling north wind and spitting snow that stung our cheeks were an ominous warning to hit for home. But we stayed. We wanted to watch for the big cans coming down ahead of the storm. Visibility was poor but we could see them and hear them, as they came over in small flocks, low and lightning fast. Suddenly, out of the swirling snow they would swish by just overhead, their wings singing like bullets. They were not dawdling. There was a desperate urgency in their rapid wing

The scouts return (Canvasbacks)
Reproduced by permission of Richard E. Bishop

Down from Manitoba (Canvasbacks)

beats as they turned it on full throttle. A dozen or more flocks whizzed past before darkness dropped a curtain on our show. But we knew these cans, fleeing before the storm, were bound for their favorite haven in this region, Lake Christina, just to the south of us. For many years, this Minnesota lake has been a rendezvous for canvasbacks during migration, and that night we knew it would be loaded with travel-weary whitebacks from the great Delta Marsh country in Manitoba.

You would think these big, smart ducks would learn their lesson and depart from the north country in decent weather. The bold ones who play around always risk the big storms that inevitably come, and it is quite common on the northern prairies to see little groups of cans huddling around small airholes in the ice on a lake—the last bits of open water. Sometimes these stubborn hangers-on are picked up by hunters, half-starved and so feeble they are unable to fly.

Being divers, the canvasbacks have a preference for the open water on larger lakes during migration and while feeding. But this does not mean they are always found there. They nest in the small prairie potholes and sloughs in the farming country and prairie lands of the northern states, and in the larger marshes of north central Canada. Their nests are well built and well con-

A welcome airhole (Canvasbacks)

cealed in the rushes, almost at water level, resting on the mud or perhaps floating in deeper water, anchored to the rushes. It's a big basketlike nest, made of dried reeds and nearby vegetation with down lining. The canvasback hen may find a number of redhead ducklings in her brood when the hatch comes off the nest, thanks to the unprincipled redhead that likes to drop its eggs in the nests of neighboring canvasbacks and thus avoid being tied down by a family of demanding youngsters.

It's fortunate that the canvasback is as hardy and patient as he is, because he is the victim of all sorts of shoddy tricks played on him by ducks of other species. The canvasback female is not only frequently stuck with rearing the young of other ducks, whose eggs she has hatched along with her own, but the entire canvasback clan unwillingly shares with other ducks much of the food they work hard to gather by diving in deep water. The baldpate duck and the common coot delight in lying in wait among the feeding cans, and when a canvasback surfaces from a dive with a bill full of wild celery or other tasty vegetation, the baldpate attacks and attempts to snatch the juicy morsels.

Fortunately, the canvasback is wary of man, or he might have been completely exterminated long ago. The first early southbound migrants in the fall were easily duped by decoys, but they learned quickly to give wide berth to every suspicious situation. However, when the latecomers were roaring down from the north, riding a wild storm, hunters would see cans dumping into their decoys with reckless abandon—any port in a storm—and this gave the hunters a heyday, filling out bag limits with whopping big, good-eating birds, fresh from the Canadian marshes.

It is not unusual during migration to see canvasback ducks flying in large, wedge-shaped flocks high overhead. What a beautiful sight they make, their white bodies, long out-stretched necks, and dark heads forming a memorable picture as they pass swiftly through the heavens and soon disappear over the horizon.

The canvasbacks follow a rather odd pattern in their fall migration. While most of them nest in the west and central prairie and marsh regions, the majority do not move directly south, but go southeast across southern Ontario, northern Minnesota, Wiscon-

(continued on page 73)

RETURNING HOME

Ruddy Duck, male *(Oxyura jamaicencis rubida)*

65

ON THEIR WAY

Ruddy Ducks (*Oxyura jamaicencis rubida*)

OVER THE MARSH

Ring-Necked Ducks (*Aythya collaris*)

67

WINGING LOW

68

Black Ducks *(Anas rubipres)*

LOOKING THINGS OVER

Blue-Winged Teal *(Anas discors discors)*

TOUCHDOWN

70

Green-Winged Teal *(Anas carolinensis)*

MOVING OUT

American Widgeon, baldpates *(Mareca americana)*

71

SPREAD FORMATION

72

Shovelers *(Spatula clypeata)*

(continued from page 64)

sin, and Michigan into the Atlantic flyway, where they like to winter in Chesapeake Bay, southern Maryland, Virginia, and the Carolinas. Others move down the Mississippi valley to the Gulf states, or west and southwest into Texas, Mexico, and along the Pacific coast.

The Greater Scaup

We have two species of scaup in North America, the greater scaup and lesser scaup. The greater scaup is a close relative of the European scaup. It so closely resembles our lesser scaup in appearance that even the experts have difficulty telling them apart. The greater scaup is larger and perhaps a quarter of a pound heavier than the lesser scaup. Both species are much better known among the hunters as bluebills or broadbills. The lesser scaup is far more numerous and much more familiar to hunters. The greater scaup is not common in either the Mississippi or Central flyways, but is quite common in the Atlantic flyway.

The habits, behavior, and migration patterns of the two scaups, however, are quite different. The greater scaup winters much farther north on both coasts, and tends to spend more time on salt water. The lesser scaup, on the other hand, keeps more to the deep south for winter, and shows less desire to go to sea in the Atlantic. The nesting range of the greater scaup is much farther north than the lesser scaup, concentrated in northwest Canada and Alaska, where it builds a typical nest on the ground near water in marshes and sloughs.

The greater scaup are marvelous divers and possess great diving power. When feeding, the scaup dives almost continuously in a tireless routine, and can remain under water for as long as a half minute. When wounded or pursued on water, it will dive and, with wings folded tightly, swim underwater with amazing speed and escape with ease. Their diet contains somewhat more aquatic animal matter than many of the diving ducks, since they feed during the winter in the coastal waters that provide all sorts of marine life scaups relish.

During migration, the greater scaup are speedy flyers and in the daytime will move over the countryside at great heights. When they lay over to rest and feed, they like to bunch up in huge rafts far out in the deeper water on large lakes. They are late nesters and seldom leave their summer homes in Alaska and northwest Canada until just ahead of the winter storms. From

73

there they travel southeast down into the Atlantic flyway, and in fewer numbers, down along the Pacific flyway. In the early winter, they seem to like the lakes and marshes of central New York. If these waters should later freeze over, they move on to sea, or scatter out along the coast farther south. On the West coast, they may winter anywhere from Aleutian Islands to southern California.

SCAUP
By Bob Hines—U.S. Dept. of Interior, Fish and Wildlife Service

The Lesser Scaup

In early spring, as you drive along the ponds and lakes about your town, perhaps the very day the ice goes out, you see all those pretty little black and white ducks scattered over the water. Some are busily diving and feeding, others quietly resting, with heads tucked under wing. From out of nowhere they seemed to suddenly appear, timing their arrival the instant the last remnants of winter ice vanished. These are the lesser scaup, a name hardly anyone calls them. We much prefer to call them "bluebills," and most hunters do. Eastern hunters call them "blackheads." These fine little ducks are always bright and early on the spring scene, impatiently pushing north from their winter homes as fast as winter retreats.

Of all our ducks, this friendly little bluebill seems least fearful of man. While migrating, it has no qualms whatsoever about dropping into the city park ponds and lakes for food and rest. In the southlands, where they winter in great masses, they become so tame they gather along shore to eagerly snap up food tossed to them by visitors.

The bluebills have always been abundant, it seems, and have provided good shooting for hunters, although most hunters have no particular desire for bluebills if there are mallards or pintails about. Unless bluebills have been gorging on fish and seafoods,

74

they are not bad eating, but hardly as delectable as the mallard and the other more highly prized ducks.

Bluebills are speedy flyers and enjoy a bit of stunting at times. They usually travel in compact flocks, and it's fun to watch them whip around a lake when they are out for a frisky exercise run.

One of my choicest memories of bluebills is a sunny October day when a friend and I were fishing from a canoe along a reedy lakeshore. We had observed a large raft of bluebills far out on the lake, and later that afternoon they rose up and took off for their daily constitutional. We could see them moving in great circles at quite a low altitude. As we watched, we saw them wheel in the sun far down the lake and head our way. They were ripping along, coming straight for us only a few feet over the water. As they drew near, we could hear the soft whistling of their wings, and I wondered if they intended to fly smack into us. Then, with wings suddenly motionless and curved, they cut a tight arc up and over our heads, barely missing us. The rush of air through their stiffened wings made a sharp, crackling roar, and they nearly blew our hats off. As they swerved away, the cut of their wings looked like flashing scimitar blades. I suspect the little scamps enjoyed buzzing us, because they made several passes at us before they had enough and went back to their feeding out on the lake. I have long since forgotten how the fishing was that day, but I will forever remember that pleasant and exciting incident with the bluebills.

The lesser scaup, or little bluebills, differ from their larger cousins, the greater scaup, in both summer and winter range. The little bluebills are widely distributed over the North American continent. They are birds of the smaller lakes, ponds, and marshes and nest much farther south than do the greater scaup. The lesser scaup's breeding range is concentrated in the northern prairie regions where most of the inland ducks nest. They nest on the ground, near the water along the edge of sloughs and marshes. Bluebills have been known to slyly drop a few eggs now and then in the nests of other species, but they're not addicted to this shabby habit as much as the redheads are.

The bluebills are great little divers and lively busybodies while feeding, always on the move, nervous and fidgety. They eat about a fifty-fifty diet of vegetation and aquatic animal matter. In fact, they'll eat just about anything, almost to the point of being called scavengers. They love to raft up on the big lakes during migration, where they mix sociably with the canvasbacks, redheads, and other diving ducks. And like all the diving ducks, when taking off to fly, they must skitter along the surface to get a running start. This handicap may be another reason why the divers like the open spaces, rather than the cozy little ponds used by the surface-feeding ducks, who can fly straight up out of the water in a twinkling.

In spite of their early arrival in the north country, the bluebills are late nesters, the very latest, in fact, with the possible exception of the white-winged scoter duck. Their broods do not hatch until early July. Since the young need ten to eleven weeks to develop flying feathers, the bluebill population is never ready to pack up for the big trip south until very late, usually just a jump ahead of a storm. Even then, they're in no hurry and take their sweet time, loafing happily along the way just a step ahead of the advancing bad weather. They winter mostly along the Gulf off the Louisiana and Florida coast. Some winter along the east and west coasts, but in much smaller numbers. The Fish and Wildlife Service reports that a million or more scaup winter on the lakes within a few miles of New Orleans.

The American Goldeneye

One raw winter day, along the rugged north shore of Lake Superior, I spotted a lively flock of handsome black and white ducks nonchalantly riding the rough open water just beyond the ice bound rocks. What manner of duck was hardy enough, or foolish enough, to challenge this uncompromising land of snow and ice at this season? None other than the energetic American, or common, goldeneye, I knew. Many of these boisterous divers, for reasons known only to themselves, elect to forego the advantages of the warmer climates and pass the winter enduring the harsh conditions that this frigid north country dishes out to both man and beast. One of the few ducks capable of existing in apparent comfort through the long northern winters is the goldeneye, also affectionately known as "whistler" and "iron head."

As I watched them bouncing among the drifting ice floes and heaving waves, they seemed oblivious to the biting cold and continued to dive and feed with joyful enthusiasm. Surely, I thought, this is a bird of unusual character. It chooses not to take the easy way of life, and then at winter's end, heads still farther north to seek out old tree cavities for its nest, rather than the usual ground

nest in the rushes. It's a duck that deserves to be admired and respected for its rugged individualism.

Not all goldeneyes remain in the north to winter. The breeding range is mainly in the far northern forest areas from Newfoundland to central Alaska, and to a lesser extent, in southern Canada and the northern states. From these nesting grounds the majority of goldeneyes migrate in small flocks, flying usually at high altitudes, and travel southwest to winter along the north Atlantic coast and eastern seaboard states. Others go west to winter along the Pacific coast from Alaska to southern California. But goldeneyes can be found throughout the winter happily settled in the northern rivers and larger lakes where open water and food are available. Somehow, they manage to find enough food to pull through.

Like the wood duck, the goldeneye prefers to nest in tree cavities and on old stumps. The nests may be as high as fifty feet from the ground. And again in the manner of the wood duck, the young goldeneye ducklings, when about two days old, must jump from the nest hole all the way down to the ground. The routine is simple. The mother calls in emphatic but reassuring tones from the ground. The youngsters, with no apparent fear, appear promptly at the nest hole and come tumbling out and down like furry balls, wildly flapping their downy wings and tiny webbed feet. Mama watches unconcernedly, and when the last of the babies hits the deck, she collects the brood and marches them off to the nearest water for their first lesson in how to be a duck.

The goldeneye is a natty black and white, with a distinctive white oval patch on its black head, between the eye and bill. This oval distinguishes the goldeneye from the Barrow's goldeneye, which has a similar patch, but crescent-shaped. Otherwise, the two species are quite difficult to tell apart.

Goldeneyes are skillful divers. If you watch them closely you will see how they dive underwater with hardly a ripple, as they seek out crabs, insects, molluscs, crustaceans, small fish, and the other aquatic life that forms most of their diet. The goldeneye is considered quite wary, but can be decoyed by skillful hunters. The meat usually has a fishy flavor, and most hunters do not regard the goldeneye as a choice duck dinner.

The wing music of goldeneyes is an interesting characteristic of these attractive birds. The penetrating whistle of their beating wings, as they rise and speed off in swift flight, is a pleasing sound that, once you hear it, you will always associate with this admirable and handsome little duck.

The Barrow's Goldeneye

Here is another rugged individualist of the duck family. This one is a mountaineer. The Barrow's goldeneye has a strong preference for the Rocky Mountains and has adopted this spectacular country as its nesting range, where it occupies tree cavities of all sorts, in the same manner as its cousin, the American goldeneye. Although it resembles the American goldeneye in both appearance and habits, it does not venture beyond the restricted region it has chosen for both nesting and wintering — the northern Rockies, the Pacific Northwest, northern California, and the southwestern coast of Canada — with one exception. The Barrow's goldeneye has established another distinct and separate nesting range in Labrador, and these eastern ducks migrate southward to winter along the north Atlantic coast. Otherwise, the Barrow's goldeneye is seldom found elsewhere on the North American continent. It has the same whistling wing music as the American goldeneye, and in many other respects the two species are very similar.

The Bufflehead Duck

After all the descriptive labels have been awarded to the more glamorous of our ducks, there remains one that is appropriate only for the diminutive bufflehead. He is "cute!" I find no word that better describes the bufflehead. With his snappy black and white dress, furry hood with white patch, pint size, and sprightly manner, this little dandy is just plain cute.

The first bufflehead I ever saw was a lone drake on a small farm pond in late spring. He was diving and feeding vigorously, apparently enjoying the luxury of a pond all to himself. When he spied me, he came up off the water with surprising speed and flashed off like a bullet. I remembered that buffleheads, although divers, can rise from the water much faster than other diving ducks. This vivacious little butterball impressed me so, I was anxious to see more of his kind. I will always regard buffleheads as the little darlings of duckdom, the teal notwithstanding.

The bufflehead is one of the smallest of ducks, almost as tiny as the teal. They are tree nesters, migrating far into the forest lands of northern and western Canada to find the necessary tree cavities and deserted woodpecker holes in which to nest. In general, the

buffleheads are small editions of the common goldeneye. They are even more skillful divers than goldeneyes, and swim very rapidly underwater in pursuit of small fish. They also have the remarkable ability to come up from under water in full flight, hardly missing a wing beat. Although they can rise quickly from the water, when landing they plop in with a belly splash and skid to a stop.

Buffleheads are very late spring migrants, the last of the divers to move out from their winter homes, which range from the Great Lakes and New England south to the Gulf of Mexico and westward to California. They are not abundant or important to hunters, but the bufflehead is a little gem of a bird to cherish as a precious part of our magnificent heritage.

The Harlequin Duck

The "clown" prince of ducks could well be the amazing Harlequin. No other duck sports such a bizarre patchwork of colors, and long ago he was appropriately named Harlequin, the actor, buffoon, the clown in his artful makeup, ready to entertain. But since this gaily decorated bird nests and winters in the cold, isolated regions of the north and along the wintry sea coasts, its beauty is seldom seen. The western subspecies has a different idea about home range and does its nesting on the western coast of Canada, and down in the Pacific Northwest, where it nests in the snowcapped mountains and frolics around in the foaming mountain torrents. Harlequin nests are built on the ground, in holes in rocks, in banks and in hollow trees. They love the cold, wave-lashed, rocky seashores, and here is where they return in winter to romp and feed almost entirely on animal matter secured by diving deep into the icy seawater.

The Ruddy and Masked Ducks

Tucked away in his own subfamily, along with a South American relative seldom seen on our shores, is a perky, bad-tempered, stiff-tailed little bird known as the ruddy duck, *Oxyura jamaicensis rubida.* In many ways he has little in common with other groups of ducks, and he holds more oddball records than all other ducks combined.

The ruddy is the only duck to raise two broods in one season. The female, though a tiny duck, hardly bigger than the teal, lays the largest of all duck eggs. Her eggs are much larger than the mallard, which is three times the size of the ruddy duck. The drake ruddy is the only duck with an air sac in the neck, which he can puff up like a toy ballon during courtship activities. Ruddy is the only duck with a bright blue bill. The male has two distinct and complete plumages, one for summer and one for winter. Ruddy males are the only ducks that assist mama in raising the brood of ducklings, and they perform the task with obvious pride.

The ruddy is so specialized for diving, with stubby legs set far astern, that it is almost helpless on land and can walk no more than a few steps before it topples over. And, though admirably equipped to submarine for fishing, it feeds mostly on plants. It is rare for any female to be silent, but the female ruddy is absolutely voiceless.

I saw a ruddy duck at close range for the first time a few years ago when I crept up on the slough near our farm one early spring morning. The slough was a popular overnight stop for travel-weary ducks, and I occasionally enjoyed sneaking up through the grass to see what the night had brought in. That morning I was surprised to see, just a few feet away near the shore, an amazing little red-brown duck with a ridiculous, unducklike tail that flared straight up like a Spanish dancer's fan. His quiet little mate was primly paddling about nearby. They were obviously preoccupied with their fantastic courtship displays, which are said to be the most spectacular of all ducks. I can believe it, because that ruddy drake put on a most amusing show. What a conceited, pompous little half-pint he was! He puffed up his chest like a strutting tom turkey, and snapped his fantail so far forward it nearly touched his head. His wide, concave bill gave him a smirky, self-satisfied look that reminded me of Walt Disney's inimitable Donald Duck. Perhaps it was the ruddy duck that inspired that famous Disney cartoon character.

For fully half an hour I watched those saucy little ruddies in amazed admiration. To my knowledge I have not seen a ruddy duck since at close range. They are rather common, but not abundant, in many areas throughout the country. They nest in the reeds and rushes along the sloughs and potholes on the northern prairies. Their principal wintering areas are on the Atlantic and Pacific coasts of the southern states. Years ago the ruddy was in great demand for its tasty meat, and the market hunters just about finished off the ruddy, until it came under the protection

of migratory waterfowl regulations. Ruddy ducks are called "boobies" on the East Coast because of their apparent disregard of a shotgun. Often when a line of ruddies is shot at they will continue the same line of flight. If shot at on the water, they can dive faster than shot will reach them.

The masked duck, *Nomonyx dominicus,* is a small duck—a very close relative of the ruddy duck and very much like the ruddy. Its habitat, however, is in South America and it is seldom seen in the United States or the North American continent.

The Old Squaw Duck

Old squaws are the winterized symbols of the subarctic regions where they nest, and the frigid northern seacoasts where they "come south" to winter. Winter is their bag, and they thrive on it. No basking in the hot sun down in the lush southlands for these happy-go-lucky little sea ducks with the long tails and curious piebald markings.

In the spring they drift far up into the Yukon and across the northern Arctic to nest on the tundras. And they don't return until the bitter cold wind, ice, and snow of winter bring them chattering and gabbling like flocks of noisy crows back to the northern seacoasts and Great Lakes. And here they are quite content to frisk merrily among the ice floes and ride the stormy waves.

The old squaws must be the gabbiest of all ducks. They have a remarkable vocabulary and all through the day keep up a continuous babbling, whether flying or on the water. They are known on the Atlantic coast as "sow southerlys" which is derived from their peculiar call that sounds like "sow-sow-southerly" and is repeated almost continuously. They fly with great speed, in small flocks,

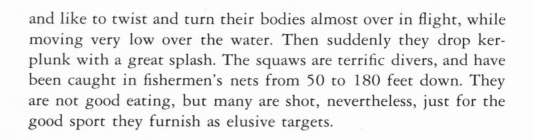

and like to twist and turn their bodies almost over in flight, while moving very low over the water. Then suddenly they drop ker-plunk with a great splash. The squaws are terrific divers, and have been caught in fishermen's nets from 50 to 180 feet down. They are not good eating, but many are shot, nevertheless, just for the good sport they furnish as elusive targets.

THE EIDER DUCKS

The eiders are among the most oceanic of all the ducks, living on the shoals off the far northern coasts and subarctic regions. Except for the American, or common eider, they usually migrate only short distances, and then only far enough south to reach open water.

There are four species of eider ducks. One of the four, the American, has four subspecies. Eiders are not commonly seen inland on the North American continent. The American eider migrates as far south as the New England coast, but seldom beyond that. The king eider is occasionally seen on the Great Lakes and both the eastern and western coasts of the United States and Canada.

The eiders' down has long been a precious commodity for its superb insulating qualities in clothing and bedding. The greedy and thoughtless slaughter of eiders for the down nearly led to their total extermination until, through provisions of the Migratory Bird Treaty for eiders, they now have the protection these beautiful birds deserve and need to survive. All of the eiders are unusually colorful. The male eiders of all species, when in full plumage, are magnificent birds. Most of the eider species are large and somewhat gooselike in shape and pose, although the legs and neck are shorter than those of geese. The female eider coloration reminds one of the mallard female.

The Steller's Eider

The Steller's eider is the smallest of the eider group — a sleek little bird in contrast to the heavy-bodied, rather awkward build of the other eiders. Its summer homeland is off the Alaska coast. In winter it may wander south a bit, as far as the Aleutian Islands. Its greatest concentration is on the Arctic coast of Siberia, westward from the Bering Straits. It positively thrives on the bitter cold weather and is happy to spend much of its time far out to sea. It nests on the ground in the flat tundras.

The Northern Eider

The northern eider is practically identical to the American or common eider and the two species often associate in both their summer and winter ranges. The northern eider range is more northerly and extends across the Arctic regions. This eider has incredible powers of endurance against the subzero temperatures, aided by the down in which its body is encased under the feathers. Its nesting habits and general behavior are much the same as those of the American eider.

The American or Common Eider

Next to the Pacific eider, the American, or common, eider is the largest of the group. With its black and white plumage, the male American eider is indeed a beautiful bird, in spite of its clumsy build. The females, as with most of the eider females, are heavily barred brown color. The American eider belongs to the species that provides the valuable down that has become such an important and useful product in the manufacture of down-insulated clothing and sleeping bags. Their ruthless persecution for generations has been brought under control and eider down is now legally produced commercially in Canada by authorization of the Canadian government.

The American eider duck flies slowly and with deliberation, usually very close to the water. It is interesting to watch them traveling along in single file, or abreast, just skimming the waves. The American eider likes to nest in chummy colonies and communities on small islands and close to salt water. The nest is simply a depression in the barren rocks, lined with weeds, sticks, grass, and down. The summer nesting range is chiefly off the coast of Labrador. In November they move down to the North Atlantic coast just far enough to reach open water. Some eiders come as far south as the coast of Massachusetts, and occasionally New Jersey.

The Pacific Eider

The Pacific eider is the largest of the eiders. In general appearance it resembles the American and northern eiders. The Arctic ranges of the Pacific and northern eiders overlap and it is thought that the two species interbreed. Nesting habits are very similar to the American eider There is very little migration movement among the Pacific eiders, except those that nest north of the Bering Straits. They must make the two-thousand-mile trip to the Aleutian Islands for the winter, as there is no open water in that distant part of the Arctic sea.

The King Eider

The king eider is another beautiful species, and, of all the eiders, it is most often found quite far south of its natural habitat. It is very abundant in the north along the Arctic coast of Alaska. King eiders are seen occasionally on the Great Lakes in winter, and on the eastern and western coasts. The king eider is probably easier to identify than the other species, with its peculiar yellow bill that extends far up on the face like an armor-plated mask. Eskimo hunters apparently relish the large fatty nob at the base of the bill and quickly remove it and eat it raw. The king eider nests in the remote subarctic regions and, unlike other eiders, prefers to nest on the mainland, often near fresh water, if available.

The Spectacled Eider

The name of the spectacled eider is well chosen. It wears a white patch around each eye, giving it the appearance of an old-time racing car driver of the Barney Oldfield era, when big goggles were standard equipment. This makes the bird easy to identify. However, most of us have never seen a spectacled eider and probably never will, because they are rare on this continent, although common in northeastern Siberia. And since American tourists have not been flocking to Siberia, the spectacled eider is one of the least known of our wildfowl. Its range is a very restricted area on the Arctic coast of Alaska.

OIL-SOAKED SCOTERS
By Bob Hines—U.S. Dept. of Interior, Fish and Wildlife Service

SCOTERS

The scoters are the large, chunky, blackish ducks commonly seen wintering along the Atlantic and Pacific coasts. The three species are all called "coots" or "sea coots" by most hunters in those regions, and they are shot in fairly large numbers more for the sport than for their meat, which is not appetizing.

All of the scoters are large ducks, with strong bony framework, tough skin, and coarse feathers very firmly attached to the skin, all of which serve them well in their ice-cold deepwater diving for food.

The White-Winged Scoter

The white-winged scoter is the most common, and the largest, of the three scoters. The drake is the only black duck on this continent with a white wing patch, which is the best means of identifying it. We see the white-winged scoters inland quite frequently, especially on the Great Lakes, during the winter months. It breeds across the span of western Canada and into Alaska, nesting on the ground in much the same manner as most other ground-nesting ducks. The white-wing flies rather laboriously, and lifts from the water with considerable effort after a long skittering run on the surface. But its air speed is deceptive and it can move with great speed. The flight is usually close to the water, just tipping the bounding waves, and usually in long stringy lines. They migrate from their nesting ranges to both seacoasts rather early in the fall, and begin returning north in March.

The American Scoter

The American scoter drake is the only American duck with entirely black plumage, coal black, with no other coloration. This, and the bright yellow-orange base of the bill are easy ways to identify the American scoter from its two cousins in this sub-family. It looks more like a duck than the other scoters. This species is the least known and least numerous of the three scoters. It is now more numerous on the Pacific coast than the Atlantic. Its principal nesting range is in the Arctic and Alaskan seaboard. The American scoter flies with more finesse than the white-wing, usually at high altitudes in good weather. Their wings make a whistling sound in flight. The American scoter is not ordinarily seen on inland water, but they do show up on the Great Lakes on occasion.

The Surf Scoter

If you will look at a picture of the male surf scoter you will see why this duck is called "skunk-head coot." Its head markings do resemble the head of a skunk. They fly in larger flocks than other scoters, and their wings create a loud humming that can be heard at considerable distance. As their name implies, surf scoters are skillful divers in the heavy surf along the coast, and employ all sorts of artful tricks to avoid being demolished by the pounding waves rolling in. The surf scoters nest in the Arctic regions, migrating southeastward and southwestward to occupy their favorite coastal bay waters along both seacoasts.

MERGANSERS

THE MERGANSERS, Subfamily Merginae
Hooded Merganser, Lophodytes cucullatus
American Merganser (common merganser)
Mergus merganser americanus
Red-breasted Merganser, Mergus serrator serrator

The interesting mergansers are a small group of three species of fish-eating ducks that inhabit the North American Continent—the hooded merganser, the American merganser, and the red-breasted merganser. They lack the usual broad and flattened bills of most ducks. For their fish-catching needs the mergansers have a long, slender, narrow, sharp-looking, almost round bill with saw-toothed edges. With this formidable equipment they can expertly seize and devour fish of considerable size. All three species have unusual and colorful plumage and both sexes are usually crested. Their long-geared and slender bodies are well adapted to their diving and rapid swimming underwater in pursuit of fish. All three species are common over great portions of North America.

The Hooded Merganser

The vivacious and colorful little hooded merganser is one of our most beautiful waterfowl. The full-plumaged drake is almost as flashy and arresting in appearance as the wood duck. In fact, the hooded merganser and wood duck have such similar nesting habits that they frequently are found in the same areas, even the same nest. The hooded is a tree nester when suitable tree cavities are available, and will fight the wood duck for a good site if necessary, or share the same nest hole if both birds can agree on that arrangement. The hooded merganser frequents the little ponds and streams. They move with amazing speed in the air and on the water. Under water they swim swiftly, using both feet and wings and it's fun to watch them pop to the surface with wiggling fish in their sharp bills. I have never known a hunter who was interested in shooting mergansers for their meat, which is tough, fishy, and quite unpalatable. The hooded nests across a wide range in the northern half of the continent and less frequently in the southern states. It winters from the Gulf of Mexico north to New England and the Great Lakes.

The American or Common Merganser

Many times, as we have paddled a canoe through the clear cold waters of the Quetico country in Ontario, little families of American, or common, mergansers have startled us witless as we came upon them suddenly around a point or ledge of rock. With a dozen or so lively ducklings trailing desperately after her, the mother clatters off across the water in a noisy fuss, indignant that their primitive solitude should be so rudely disturbed. Like the loon, these beautiful mergansers are very much a part of this wild and still primitive north country where they come to nest and rear their young. I love to see and watch these pretty and graceful waterfowl lending their color to this picturesque land of the voyageur. I somehow resent the inelegant name of "fishduck" which they are frequently called by both hunters and fishermen, neither of whom have a high regard for the mergansers in general. Fishermen accuse mergansers of gobbling up many small game fish. Admittedly, the mergansers are expert fishers, but there has never been sufficient scientific research or evidence to prove or disprove either side of the argument. As for me, I will take the mergansers and they are welcome to some of our fish. A small price to pay for having these delightful waterfowl on our lakes and streams.

This species is the largest of the mergansers, and the best diver of the group, almost as good as the loon. The American, or common, merganser is well distributed throughout North America, but shows more preference for the fresh inland waters than does the red-breasted merganser. We find it often in open waters on lakes and streams long after freeze-up and deep into winter. The nesting range covers the northern portion of the continent and well up into the subarctic.

There's some question about this merganser's nesting habits. Does it nest in tree cavities, or on the ground? Apparently it nests in quite a variety of places, including tree holes, on the ground among driftwood, among boulders, in dense woods and brush, or under the low thick branches of pine and spruce trees. Old nests of crows and hawks may also be used.

Migration of the common mergansers in the spring begins very early from their wintering areas around the Great Lakes, along both coasts from the far north to the southern states.

This American merganser is facetiously called by gunners "Irish canvasback." They do resemble canvasbacks at a distance except for their green heads.

The Red-Breasted Merganser

The red-breasted merganser has many of the traits and behavior patterns of the other mergansers, especially the American. However, unlike the others, the red-breasted is definitely a ground nester, and shows a preference for wintering on the seacoasts. It is quite common throughout the northern portions of the United States and Canada, but probably less abundant than the American species. The red-breasted female and American merganser female are very similar in appearance and quite difficult to tell apart. But the red-breasted has a straggly double crest, while the American merganser female has a rather thin single crest. These ducks, like all mergansers, are great divers and catch great quantities of fish and other aquatic life.

RED-BREASTED MERGANSERS
By Bob Hines—U.S. Dept. of Interior, Fish and Wildlife Service

Forming the V (Canada Geese)

THE GEESE

THE GEESE OF NORTH AMERICA Subfamily Anserinae

Common Canada goose, Branta canadensis canadensis
Western Canada goose, Branta canadensis occidentalis
Lesser Canada goose, Branta canadensis leucopareia
Richardson's goose, Branta canadensis hutchinsi
Cackling goose, Branta canadensis minima
American brant, Branta bernicla hrota
Black brant, Brant nigricans
Barnacle goose, Branta leucopsis (not native in North America)
Emperor goose, Philacte canagica
White-fronted goose, Anser albifrons albifrons
Tule goose, Anser albifrons gambelli
Lesser snow goose, Chen hyperborea hyperborea
Greater snow goose, Chen hyperborea atlantica
Blue goose, Chen caerulescens
Ross's goose, Chen rossi

When the moon is full on an early spring night, and suddenly the melodious cry of geese passing high overhead comes drifting down, we listen with almost joyous rapture. For this is the wild sweet music of assurance that the long and dreary cold of winter will soon be gone. No wonder that generations of country folk have loved these winged prophets of spring as they sweep majestically through the heavens, their clarion calls spreading the good news.

The geese are a large group, about thirty-five forms, widely distributed throughout the world and varying greatly in color and size. On the North American continent we have about fifteen forms if we include the European barnacle goose, which is an infrequent visitor to the eastern seaboard, and not native to this continent.

There is much disagreement among the ornithologists over the scientific naming and identification of the various forms of the Canada goose. The classification we use here may or may not be acceptable to the authorities, but it is a compromise that will suffice for the purpose of this book. Meanwhile, the geese, unconcerned as to their Latin nomenclature, will continue in the same old familiar patterns that these wonderful birds have followed down through the centuries.

Geese form a natural link between the swans and ducks. The length of neck and size of body are generally intermediate between the swans and ducks. In most species of geese the sexes are alike in color. Being better walkers than either swans or ducks, geese are enthusiastic land feeders and like to graze like herds of cattle on grass and other greens, as well as farmers' grain, corn, berries, and nuts. When they're winging their way across the thousands of miles they must cover on migration, it takes a lot of eating to keep their enormous appetites satisfied, and many a farmer pays a stiff price in damaged fields once the hungry geese have paid his land a visit. When feeding on water, geese perform much the same as the surface-feeding ducks, stretching their necks down in the shallow places, and tipping, tail up, in search of food underwater.

All geese are tremendously powerful flyers and cover immense distances on their annual migrations from nesting grounds, which can be from within the Arctic circle, to their winter homes in the far south. The geese are still numerous up and down the flyways every spring and fall, but their population is pitifully small compared to the unbelievable millions of them that moved through the skyways many, many years ago before our onrushing civilization began its relentless toll.

The Common Canada Goose

There are five varieties or subspecies of the Canada goose. Their habits and characteristics are all similar, but they do exhibit great racial variations in size and relative proportions. They also differ in distribution. The Canada goose is the big game of North American waterfowl, the kings, aristocrats and lords of the skyways — and a rich prize for the hunter having the skill or good fortune to bring this tasty bird to bag.

Regardless of size and color variations in the different subspecies of the Canada goose, the hallmark of the clan is the black-stockinged neck and head, with prominent white cheek patches. All Canada geese are wily, cunning, alert, strong and practice an admirable code of fidelity. In many respects the Canada goose could well serve as a model of wisdom and behavior for man.

Winging along (Canada Geese)
Reproduced by permission of Richard E. Bishop

The grandest of all the five subspecies is the common Canada goose. My appreciation for the sagacity of this noble bird first developed when I was nine years old, and living on an Iowa farm. A great clamoring throng of these beautiful geese came winging over our farmhouse early one fall evening. They were moving very slowly, barely clearing the treetops, and making a great fuss. There were hundreds of them—an exciting and unforgettable sight. Obviously, they were preparing to settle down and have an all-night picnic in a nearby field of corn not yet picked. The din of their gabbling must have been audible for miles. No sooner had the last goose dropped out of sight among the tall cornstalks than a neighboring farmer came running up the road, shotgun in hand. He had a goose dinner in mind. We watched in suspenseful anticipation as he climbed the fence and began his stalk down the corn rows. But our neighbor was unskilled in the lore of goose hunting and had not reckoned with the craftiness of this canny bird he sought. The geese, we knew, were some distance into the field. But the eager hunter had proceeded no more than a few paces when a huge gander—one of many no doubt standing guard around the feeding flock—sounded the alarm and sprang into the air almost from under the startled farmer's feet. The gander's shrill warning cry instantly brought a thousand geese thundering up from the field like a giant, flopping carpet, far out of gun range. In a moment they were gone. We listened a long time to their complaining voices as they drifted like a dark cloud into the dusk of the western sky. My dad chuckled. Knowing the ways of geese, it had turned out just as he expected. There would be no goose dinner for our neighbor. I could not feel sorry for him. I felt only deep admiration for Canada geese, and gladness that their Creator had endowed them with such cunning ways. It may have been the cherished memory of this incident early in life, but somehow I have never had the hunter's burning desire to kill one of these noble waterfowl. Just to see them and thrill to their wild calling is enough.

The common Canada goose is a huge fellow, with a wing spread as much as five feet, and weighing from eight to thirteen pounds. With their beautiful gray-brown bodies and the familiar black neck and head with white cheek patches, they are unmistakable in the air or on the water. The Canada is affectionately known everywhere as "honker" in deference to his stentorian, resonant honk-onk-aonk—the stirring bugle call that floats down from their high-flying V's in the heavens, the welcome notes announcing spring's arrival. How their clarion call fills us with awe at the mystic power that impels them! Except for the weird laughter of the loon on a northern lake, I know of no other bird call so thrilling, so filled with the spirit of the wilderness.

The common Canada is the only goose seen in many localities, and during migration, it appears in most states at some season of the year. They breed across Canada and Alaska, with smaller, localized wild breeding populations still existing in the northern states. Newly established flocks are now developing in many sections of the United States. The common Canada goose, for all its wariness, is easily domesticated, and many are raised by game breeders and conservation departments for stocking purposes.

The Canada goose mates for life. It is said that when either partner dies or is killed the survivor never pairs again, but this a theory that has neither been proved nor disproved. The gander is a fierce and formidable contender for a mate during courtship, and the battle between two rival ganders is a crunching duel that the whole flock gathers round to witness.

The nests are usually on the ground near water. They are bulky piles of reeds, sticks, and weeds, well lined with down. Unlike most waterfowl, the gander does not desert his brooding mate, but stands by staunchly and fearlessly defending the nest from all intruders and predators. He is a vicious fighter and can deliver a crushing blow with his powerful wings, and many an animal, as well as man, has been clobbered within an inch of his life by one of these aroused ganders. This tough, wild fellow can beat off a fox or any other animal he thinks is coming too close for safety.

During the spring and summer, the Canada geese feed on a great variety of insects, plant leaves, berries, seeds, and aquatic roots. They are vegetarians, but will eat small crustaceans of different sorts when necessary. But their first love in food is the farmers' grain fields across the prairies. Here they like to graze in huge flocks across the stubble and corn fields in the fall. Most of these geese move south for the winter, occupying open water in many regions, from Nova Scotia, British Columbia and along both coasts of the United States.

The Western Canada Goose

The western Canada goose is a darker colored edition of the common Canada, and apart from being nonmigratory, its habits, behavior, and size seem to be identical with those of the common

Mates (Canada Geese)

Canada goose. It occupies a definitely local habitat from Vancouver Island, in British Columbia, north to Prince William Sound, in Alaska. It rarely wanders inland at any season.

The Lesser Canada Goose

For many years prior to 1931, the lesser Canada goose was improperly identified as "Hutchins's Goose." The Hutchins's goose was a very small goose discovered in 1831 in Hudson Bay, and was named after a man called Hutchins, with the Hudson's Bay Company. Somehow, the little goose was forgotten and the name was later mistakenly applied to a small version of the Canada goose. This confusion was rectified in 1931 by the American Ornithological Union, and now we have the lesser Canada goose and the Richardson's goose, the new name for the Hutchins's. The lesser Canada is a short-necked replica of the common Canada goose. Its breeding range is along the extreme northern Arctic coasts. It winters, in large numbers, in the interior valley of California, in association with white-fronted geese, cackling geese, lesser snows, and Ross's geese. The habits and behavior, otherwise, are much the same as the Canada goose.

Richardson's Goose

Richardson's goose is the little goose of the Arctic region, discovered by Sir John Richardson, and for many years it was called Hutchins's goose. Now renamed Richardson's, it is a dead ringer for the common Canada, but much smaller. Its breeding range and migration pattern differ from the other Canada geese. It breeds in the eastern Arctic and migrates down Hudson Bay and through southern Manitoba, Nebraska, Iowa, the Dakotas, and the Mississippi valley, wintering on the northern gulf coast of Mexico.

The Cackling Goose

The cackling goose is the smallest subspecies of the Canada goose, and, like the western Canada goose, is a darker colored variety of the species. The cackling goose is also a westerner in its winter range, using the same interior valley country of California as the lesser Canada geese, snows, white-fronts and Ross's. It derives its name from the shrill chicken-like call that is repeated over and over. Their breeding range is restricted to the Yukon-Kuskokwim Delta of Alaska.

THE BRANT

There are two species of brant common in North America, and both are similar in appearance, behavior, and food habits. The American brant is the Atlantic subspecies and differs from the black brant of the Pacific coast variety mainly in coloration. The American brant has a lighter breast. Both are small, slightly larger than a mallard.

BRANT IN FLIGHT
By Bob Hines—U.S. Dept. of Interior, Fish and Wildlife Service

The American Brant

The American (white-bellied) brant is a true sea-goose, and is rarely seen away from salt water. The attractive brant was a favorite game bird along the Atlantic coast until 1931, when it almost became extinct because its principal food, eelgrass, suddenly was wiped out by disease. Those brants that managed to survive switched their diet to sea lettuce and have since been slowly increasing in numbers. However, the sea lettuce taints the meat, so the brant has lost status with the hunters. Now the eelgrass has returned to the Atlantic bays and the brant are increasing.

It is estimated that the brant population on the Atlantic coast is now 150,000 to 200,000 birds. The well-developed salt glands of the brant enable them to drink sea water and eat coastal plants. But during their three-month nesting season on the eastern Arctic coast they are land grazers and prefer fresh water, although they are never far from the sea. The brant have many enemies that prey on them and their nests. The Arctic fox has been the most destructive predator. Snowy owls, jaegers, wolves, herring gulls, all are predators that take a heavy toll of brant eggs and young.

As the wings of young brant develop, the families abandon the nesting grounds and gather in large flocks along the coast near tide flats and lagoons, lush with food plants. When snow and freeze-up time comes they move out and come down to the Atlantic coast in the vicinity of New Jersey for the winter.

The Black Brant

The black brant is the Pacific brant, and similar in habits, behavior, and size to the Atlantic edition, or American brant. The black brant is so-called because of its dark breast in contrast to the light-breasted American brant. The black brant nests farther west in the Arctic regions in the Yukon-Kuskokwin Delta and coasts of Siberia and western Arctic Canada. In migrating southward for the winter, the blacks fly directly to northern California.

The White-Fronted Goose

The white-fronted goose is another true westerner that likes the wide open spaces, and is rarely seen in the eastern half of the continent. They breed in the trackless Arctic prairies in the summer, and when moving south to their favorite winter resort in the inland refuges of central California, and coastal marshes of Mexico, Texas, and Louisiana, the white-fronts fly over the western areas which supply ample elbow room for feeding and resting. Many know the white-front as speckle-belly or gray-wavey. He is a choice bird in the roaster, better eating, many claim, than the vaunted Canada goose. The white-fronted goose is so-named because it has a white forehead and forecrown, which are distinctive marks. It is a medium sized bird, and primarily a grazer, but when the opportunity comes, he will fill his gizzard with corn, wheat, barley, or rice. White-fronts have a high-pitched tootling call that resembles laughter.

The Tule Goose

The tule goose is a subspecies and larger edition of the white-fronted goose. The two are identical except for size and the darker coloration of the tule. Its breeding grounds have never been definitely known, although some years ago tules were found nesting in the Canadian Arctic on a large, nameless lake near the Perry River. The tules winter chiefly in Butte, Colusa, and Sutter counties of California. There is grave concern among conservationists that the tule may be nearing extinction, as there are fewer reports on it each year.

The Barnacle Goose

The Barnacle goose is a European salt-water species that shows up occasionally on the Atlantic seaboard. But it is not native on this continent and is therefore almost an accidental species. It has a close resemblance to the American brant and Canada goose, and is told from the American brant by the white head, and from the Canada by the white forehead and black chest. There is no record of them nesting on this continent. Their breeding grounds are in Greenland and Spitzbergen.

EMPEROR GEESE STALKED BY ALASKAN BROWN BEAR
By Bob Hines—U.S. Dept. of Interior, Fish and Wildlife Service

The Emperor Goose

There may be as many as two hundred thousand emperor geese on the continent, but they are rarely seen, either by hunters or naturalists. The winter and summer range is confined to sparsely settled and uninhabited lands bordering the Bering Sea. It stays far from centers of human population, even in migration. There are records, however, of the emperor goose appearing occasionally all along the western Pacific coast to California. The emperor is as much a sea goose as the brant, and frequents rocks, reefs, shoals of salt, and brackish lagoons, but becomes a land bird during nesting season. The emperor is a beautiful bird, with its gray body heavily barred in black and white, yellow legs and feet, and white head, touched with dashes of rusty red. They are subjected to many predators, including the Eskimos, who trap many of them for food and rob the nests of eggs. But, like other geese, they somehow survive and adapt to even the worst conditions.

The Snow Geese

One of the prettiest sights in our natural world is a long wavy line of snow geese overhead, their lovely white wings, tipped with jet black, beating rhythmically against the cobalt blue of a clear fall sky, as they float southward, their falsetto music trailing faintly after them. We watch them with a touch of sadness. Going north they were happy harbingers of spring, but now their southbound journey means that winter draws near. As their name—hyperborea—suggests, from the north wind they come. It is possible that the lesser geese are the most abundant of all geese on this continent. These are large pure white birds with black wing tips, smaller in size than the Canada, and easily identified when mingling with other species of geese.

There are two species of the snows. The lesser snow is the more abundant, more widespread in its wintering grounds, inclined to favor the western half of the United States.

There are blue goose phases of the lesser snow goose, which makes this species a very confusing one, and naturalists do not seem to agree on how the lessers, greaters and blue phases should be classified. The snow geese and blue geese apparently interbreed freely, and there are many family groups that include both colors and various phases of color. The greater snow geese have no blue phases.

Anyone who likes to watch the spring migration of geese can see thousands of lesser snow geese as well as blue and Canada geese, on the prairies of the Dakotas as they come up through the Mississippi flyway from the south in early spring. Spectacular flocks of migrating snows and blues take their time, loafing along following the retreating snow and ice, resting on the sloughs and potholes, and feeding in the stubble and corn fields. They are carefully watched and guarded all the way from their winter homes up to the Canadian border, by special patrols of federal game wardens whose round-the-clock job is to keep an eye on these flocks and protect them from the inevitable poachers and any other hazards that might endanger these precious birds.

The snow geese like to nest close to each other, and naturalists have reported finding nesting concentrations of twelve hundred pairs of snow geese to the square mile.

The greater snow goose is identical to the lesser snow goose, except it is generally larger, chunkier with thicker neck, and larger bill and head. The greater snow goose is exclusively a bird of the Atlantic coast and seldom invades the interior. They concentrate for wintering in the Chesapeake Bay- Currituck Sound area of Maryland, Virginia and North Carolina. However, large concentrations of big snows have been observed in Cameron Parish, Louisiana. In the spring they migrate far northward to nest in northern Greenland and the more northerly part of the Arctic Archipelago of Canada.

The Blue Goose

In the blue goose we have all the mystery, the wild freedom and blue distances that we associate with our high wandering waterfowl. Indeed, for many years the blue goose was truly a scientific mystery whose pilgrimages into the unknown regions of the Arctic wilderness baffled ornithologists. Finding the nesting range of the blue goose was an alluring challenge that was at last accomplished by J. Dewey Soper, who found the distinctive blues nesting on the western tundra of Baffin Island. Later, another nesting area was found on Hudson Bay, where the lesser snow goose is also found, and the two occasionally interbreed.

The blue goose is medium sized with a pretty dusky-gray and brown body, white head and neck. But we see them in all sorts of hybrid color mixtures as a result of their cross-breeding with the lesser snows, and hardly a flock of snow or blue geese comes over the flyway, spring or fall, that is not peppered with these mixtures.

The Baffin Island tundra is a vast and desolate land of sodden marshes, mud flats, and everlasting ice—a gloomy land haunted by leaden skies and harrassed by chilling gales of rain and snow. Into this land the young blue goose is born and raised to take his part in the long fall flight to the softer climate of his winter home on the coast of Louisiana.

During their spring migration from the gulf coast, the blues move up the Mississippi flyway in great concentrations, accompanied by many snow geese. They linger on the Dakota prairies, then drive northeast to their rendezvous in the barren land of Baffin. In the fall, however, they fly on a direct course southwest, straight for Louisiana, which must look very good to them after the miserable unpleasantness of a summer in Baffin.

The Ross's Goose

The Ross's goose is a beautiful little snow-white goose, closely resembling the lesser snow goose, but much smaller. The Ross's is about the size of a mallard and considered the smallest of all geese. The Ross's goose nests in Arctic Canada, near the Perry River, and winters in the valleys of the Sacramento and San Joaquin rivers in central California.

THE SWANS

Think what an awesome spectacle it must have been, when only the American Indian inhabited this land, to see a thousand swans, in wavering V-shaped wedges, sweeping majestically through the sky, great snowy wings beating a slow steady rhythm, their trumpet-calling filling the prairie with a restless, haunting music. The early explorers, as they pushed westward, gazed upon these massive flights of swans and found the wonder and drama of it all beyond their power to describe.

The stately swans have always been universal symbols of beauty and graceful movement. They have influenced and inspired mankind's history, art, drama, music, literature, and folklore. But the swans have paid a dear price for their beauty. Their size made them tempting targets, and their lovely plumage brought a handsome price on the London market for women's fashions. Years of wanton persecution brought the once abundant trumpeter very near the point of extinction. Only a meager remnant of the once enormous swan flocks remains.

The three species of swans in North America all look very much alike. The mute swan is not native, but a European import. Since colonial times this has been the ornamental bird seen on our park lagoons and ponds.

The whistling swan is the most numerous, presently numbering between seventy and ninety thousand, wildlife authorities say.

The trumpeter is the largest of the three species. For years it has been fighting an uphill struggle to maintain its existence in competition with man's modern world, and were it not for the careful protection it has been getting in special refuges, the trumpeter would have become extinct long ago.

Both whistling and trumpeter swans resemble each other so closely it is very difficult to tell them apart. The sexes are identical in coloring. The adults are pure white, with black feet and legs. Whistlers are usually smaller than trumpeters and generally can be identified by a small yellow streak dropping like a tear just below the eye. However, on some whistlers this mark is not always evident; then your guess is as good as anybody's, unless you hear their voice. With their long necks, short powerful legs, and huge webbed feet, the swans are well equipped to forage for their food in shallow water in much the same manner as the surface-feeding ducks. They poke around under the water with their long, angular necks — eating leaves, stems, seeds, and tubers of plants. They use their feet to dig and claw in the mucky marsh and slough bottoms to loosen roots and tubers and stir up whatever vegetation is available. Swans do not move about much on land to graze, as geese do, and seldom go ashore except to nest. The male swan is called a cob and the female is called a pen. The young are cygnets.

On the water, the whistler and trumpeter swans carry the neck erect and the bill horizontal. The mute swan arches the neck and points the bill downwards.

To all these noble birds that have been so much a part of our history we have a responsibility of continued vigilance and determination to preserve and perpetuate them for the enjoyment and enrichment of future generations.

The Whistling Swan

When the frosty nights of autumn are turning the vast northern tundra to browns, reds, and golds, the whistling swans begin to assemble in great concentrations on the lakes, ponds, and marshes of the Alaskan and Canadian wilderness. As many as twenty-five thousand may gather on a single lake or marsh. For several days they spend sociable hours preening, oiling, and carefully arranging their beautiful white feathers. Occasionally small flocks wheel out over the marsh in short practice flights. Everywhere among the flocks there is an air of excitement, expectation, and serious preparation. They know the time is near for the long, grueling journey south, and they talk about it incessantly in their high nasal voices.

Then one clear, cold morning their clamor grows to a hysterical pitch. This is the day and they are impatient. "What's holding us up? Let's get going!" they seem to scream to their leaders. Suddenly a small family group lifts off the marsh and heads straight south. Another flock quickly follows, then another and another. In rapid succession flock after flock takes off and joins the others. Soon they are gone from sight, and the marsh lies empty and silent except for the chill wind that riffles the water and rattles the dry grass.

Up and up the flying wedges and white, floating ribbons climb

(continued on page 113)

THE SENTINEL

Common Canada Geese *(Branta canadensis canadensis)*

105

WINGING IN

Common Canada Geese *(Branta canadensis canadensis)*

HEADED SOUTH

Common Canada Geese *(Branta canadensis canadensis)*

107

SOLITARY LANDING

Trumpeter Swan *(Olor buccinator)*

FLIGHT FORMATION

Common Canada Geese *(Branta canadensis canadensis)*

OVER THE SURF

110

Whistling Swans *(Olor columbianus)*

BEACHCOMBERS

Snow Geese *(Chen hyperborea hyperborea)*

111

HIGH FLYERS

112

Blue Geese *(Chen caerulescens)*

(continued from page 104)

until they are barely visible from the ground. At the head of each detachment a venerable whistler cob leads, barking out commands like a tough old drill sergeant, trying to keep rambunctious young cygnets in their proper places. On and on they drive, thousands of feet above the green carpeted wilderness below.

WHISTLING SWANS
By Bob Hines—U.S. Dept. of Interior,
Fish and Wildlife Service

All along the way flocks drop down from their high wandering to rest and feed on large lakes where they have stopped many times in years past. To the older swans these resting stops and the wintering grounds are familiar scenes. Some have traveled these skyways for as long as a quarter-century—perhaps longer, for swans are known to be long-lived. In captivity, they have lived as long as thirty-two years.

Perhaps half of the migrating swan flocks will veer southeast, bound for the Atlantic coast, the shallow estuaries of Chesapeake Bay, and the countless inlets from Maryland to South Carolina. Others will stop at their favorite winter resort, the Bear River Refuge in northern Utah, and still others will spend their winter along the Pacific coast and in the central valley of California.

Some years ago I had the delightful experience of seeing a dozen or so whistlers sail very low over our house while reconnoitering for a landing on the nearby lake. I was in the yard when I looked up and was astonished to see them coming directly for me, just over the treetops. They made no sound except the whoosh-whoosh of their huge wings. They seemed like white airships, their long necks reaching out like straight white ropes with a black dot of a head at the end. They passed slowly over the house, circled, and, satisfied that the lake was satisfactory, slanted down into a long glide, pitching onto the water's glassy surface with hardly a ripple. That night I could hear their wow-ou-wow and who-who calls as they rested and dabbled after their day's journey north. The next morning I hurried down to the lakeshore hoping to see them, but they were gone, soaring a mile high, no doubt, somewhere far to the north. The lake is in the heart of a big city, and since wary swans prefer the remote places, I thought this visit was a rather rare and remarkable event.

The whistling swan is the most common species of the three on this continent. They are much more numerous than the trumpeter and in no immediate danger of extinction. In contrast to the trumpeter, the whistler's wariness and the remoteness of its summer home have helped preserve its numbers.

In flight the whistler and the trumpeter are easily recognized by the snow-white body, long outstretched neck, and large white wings that seem to move slowly. But those impressive wings con-

113

vey a feeling of surging, driving power. The swans fly faster than either ducks or geese.

The call of whistling swans is one means of distinguishing them from the trumpeters. The whistler sounds a high-pitched barklike wow-ou-wow and a who-who. The trumpeter's call is mellow and hornlike. A flock of trumpeters whooping it up sounds like all the French horn players from a dozen symphony orchestras trying to get in tune, and doing a bad job of it.

When pitching into the water, swans do not usually extend their feet in front, as the geese and ducks do. With feet retracted, they glide easily into the water with a belly landing like an amphibious plane, so gracefully and lightly they barely make a splash. To take off, they must face into the wind, just as aircraft do, and make a short, pattering run along the surface for fifteen or twenty feet before clearing. For such a large bird this is a very quick lift-off compared to the longer runs that many of the geese and diving ducks must make.

Whistlers nest over a wide area from Alaska to Baffinland. With some exceptions, they scatter widely and thinly, keeping to themselves in the remote areas. All swans pair for life, but the whistler does not mate until its third year. For a nest they build up a two-foot mound of grass, moss, and sedge, preferably on top of the low hills back from the water's edge a half-mile or so. Four eggs is the usual clutch, and they incubate in about thirty-two days. The cygnets hatch late in June or early in July, if the weather is normal.

Nesting swans are very jealous of their territories, and each pair stakes out a relatively large claim. They will tolerate ducks but will chase off larger trespassers, such as geese and other swans.

The young cygnets face many hazards, and fatalities are so frequent that on the average only two or three in a nest will survive to fly south in autumn. When spring is late and winter comes early on the nesting grounds, some cygnets may still be flightless at freeze-up. These poor things must be left behind by the migrating flocks to perish from the cold and starvation.

The Trumpeter Swan

The trumpeter swan is one of our most magnificent waterfowl, and a spectacular creature to watch as it moves through the sky with incredible speed and grace. What a wretched indictment

Checking the territory (Trumpeter Swans)
Reproduced by permission of Richard E. Bishop

of man's greed and thoughtless disregard for our wildlife inheritance that this once-abundant fowl is almost a vanishing race. The swans are not prolific, and once their numbers are diminished, several generations of undisturbed peace are required to restore them.

Life for the trumpeter in our modern world has been disastrous. They are not as shy and distrustful of man as the whistling swans, and their tendency to inhabit the more precarious southerly ranges has made them vulnerable to the many hazards of civilization. Whistlers, on the other hand, summer as far north as possible. They choose the remotest areas, and this explains their greater abundance today. The trumpeter has another inherent weakness in its habit of traveling overland in small family groups and cruising along shorelines where it is an easy target. They have been much too trusting for their own good. But now that they are getting careful protection and have been provided sanctuary in a number of favorable refuge areas, the trumpeters are slowly coming back in increasing numbers.

Trumpeters once ranged and nested throughout the north, west, and central parts of North America, from Alaska and Arctic Canada, south to Iowa, Missouri and Indiana. Many wintered along the Ohio and Mississippi river valleys, and in the fresh water inlets along the Gulf of Mexico. The only trumpeters we have now are descendants of those lucky ones that escaped the hunters or did not migrate long distances. Very limited numbers now nest in Alaska, British Columbia, Alberta, and Saskatchewan. Other small groups are populating the several refuges in the United States and Canada, where they receive full protection the year around.

Trumpeters nesting in the more southerly regions like to nest on top of muskrat houses. If no accommodating muskrats are around, they build a nesting mound of reeds and vegetation. It's a huge affair — four or five feet across at the bottom — and looks like a haystack. The hen will usually lay an average of five or six eggs. Some years, as many as half of the eggs fail to hatch, and this further handicaps the trumpeter in its uphill comeback to a normal population. Then, after hatching, some of the cygnets are trampled to death by awkward parents who are not as graceful on land as in the water. Other cygnets, on their first venture into the water to feed, become entangled in weeds and drown. Parasites of all kinds prey on the young, and the weak birds die quickly. As with all birds, the early days in the life of cygnets are indeed full of many dangers and uncertainties.

Those trumpeters nesting in Alberta apparently move south in the fall with the last of the whistlers coming through. The trumpeters nesting in Alaska fly out to the coastal lakes and rivers of southeasterly Alaska and British Columbia, or if the winter is very severe they may come even farther south.

Recently, along the Madison River in Yellowstone National Park, we watched several pairs of trumpeters moving about on the water in the stately manner of all swans. They paid no heed to us, although they were quite near the highway as we drove along paralleling the river. One trumpeter took off and sailed just over our car. He seemed to want to race us down the road, for he kept just above and ahead of us for almost a mile. His great wings beat a slow, steady, lazy-looking rhythm, but their tremendous power drove the trim white form at a speed we could not match at the legal speed limit. What a memorable picture of graceful motion he made coursing his way through the majestic valley of the Madison.

The Mute Swan

The mute swans were brought to this country from Europe in early colonial days and have been very much a part of our culture and history. It is usually the mute swan we see moving with solemn dignity about our park ponds and lagoons. The mute looks very much like the whistling and trumpeter swans, and the most distinctive difference is the mute's reddish bill, and the large black knob at the base of the male's bill. The mute usually holds its neck in a graceful arch with the bill pointed down. The whistler and trumpeter usually carry the neck erect. The mute is not entirely mute. It does not have a loud clarion call, as do the other swans, but it can give out with an angry hiss to frighten off intruders, and in calling its cygnets can make a sound somewhat like the bark of a small pup. It is the mute swan that, according to legend, sets its wings when mortally wounded and glides to the water singing a strange and haunting "swan song." This is purely legend, never scientifically verified, but it is apparently the source of the common expression, "singing the swan song." Several hundred mute swans, escapees from captivity in the parks no doubt, are naturalized and now in a wild state along the coast from New Jersey to Massachusetts.

THE MYSTERY OF MIGRATION

When the glorious music of the migrant wild geese drifts down from on high, you watch their wavering lines pass over and on into the distance, wondering, as men have for centuries, what mystic power impels them and guides them unerringly on their course.

The migration of birds has been a tantalizing puzzle for thousands of years. From the very beginning mankind was baffled by the regular and sudden appearance and disappearance of the birds and wildfowl. The Bible, in Jeremiah 8:7, acknowledges the scheduled arrivals and departures of the birds: "Yea, the stork in the heaven knoweth her appointed times; and the turtle [dove] and the crane and the swallow observe the time of their coming . . ." Surely the North American Indian, dependent upon game for his livelihood, was keenly aware that the birds and waterfowl deserted the colder regions at summer's end to return in the spring.

Down through the centuries learned men of science, and others perhaps not so learned, have expounded many amazing and intriguing theories and labored over ingenious experiments attempting to solve the riddle of migration. Some of these pronouncements were utterly ridiculous, such as the one that had birds going into hibernation in secret places, or the one claiming they flew to the moon in sixty hours to hibernate.

But from all the delving and groping no infallible answers have come, no profound wisdom extracted from the years of wondering. So we go on, still seeking and questioning.

How do birds find their way across the continents and the trackless oceans? On what curious compass do they rely for their sense of direction? Is their orientation based on the earth's rotation? Are they influenced by cosmic rays? Do celestial bodies, the sun or stars, serve as beacons to guide them? Do they possess some innate terrestrial map of continental checkpoints to keep them from straying? How do they know when to begin their seasonal pilgrimages? How does a duck or goose know its home or breeding territory, perhaps thousands of miles away, after an absence of several months?

The food patrol (Bluebills)
Reproduced by permission of Richard E. Bishop

What started birds migrating in the first place? Ornithologists point out that the birds of the northern hemisphere are the most migratory, and this suggests that the ice sheets during the Pleistocene epoch may have been originally responsible. The birds were forced south ahead of the advancing glaciers — then followed them back when the glaciers receded. Now, each winter is like a brief recurrence of the ice age, with the birds retreating to their ancestral resorts in the south and returning when the snow and ice have gone. While the idea seems to make sense, it does not explain migration in many parts of the world that were never touched by glaciation. Many authorities reject this theory and believe that birds have been migrating for millions of years, long before the Pleistocene epoch.

Migration is the greatest adventure in the life of a bird. It encounters many hazards in its short lifetime, but none compare with the dangerous risks involved in migration. Every year millions of migrants fail to reach their destinations. Day and night the airborne travelers must contend with natural and man-made perils — storms, fog, ice, wind, shortage of food or resting places. Night flyers collide with television towers, tall buildings, and lighted structures. All conspire to take a ghastly toll of birds as they ply their way.

It is not likely that birds and waterfowl have a built-in weather forecasting system, as some people believe. One theory advanced is that when the time comes for their departure north or south, they seem to be triggered by the barometric pressure and other meteorological conditions prevailing at the time their journey begins. There is another theory that birds are prompted to start migrating at about the same time each year by significant glandular changes. The change may be influenced by light — increasing light in the spring and decreasing light in the fall. When the day arrives, the bird, for reasons it cannot possibly know or understand, leaves for its distant goal. The trouble with this theory is that birds wintering in the southern hemisphere are experiencing decreasing day lengths, rather than increasing, in the period before migrating. All these factors are so complex as to be the despair of scientists, and none is wholly accepted by ornithologists or researchers.

Waterfowl prepare themselves for migration well in advance. Both ducks and geese begin by donning a new or partly new suit of clothing. If they customarily travel great distances, they lay in a supply of fuel in the form of fat under the skin. They preen, oil, and carefully arrange their feathers for days before the journey

AVERAGE DISTRIBUTION OF NORTH AMERICAN
BREEDING AND WINTERING DUCKS

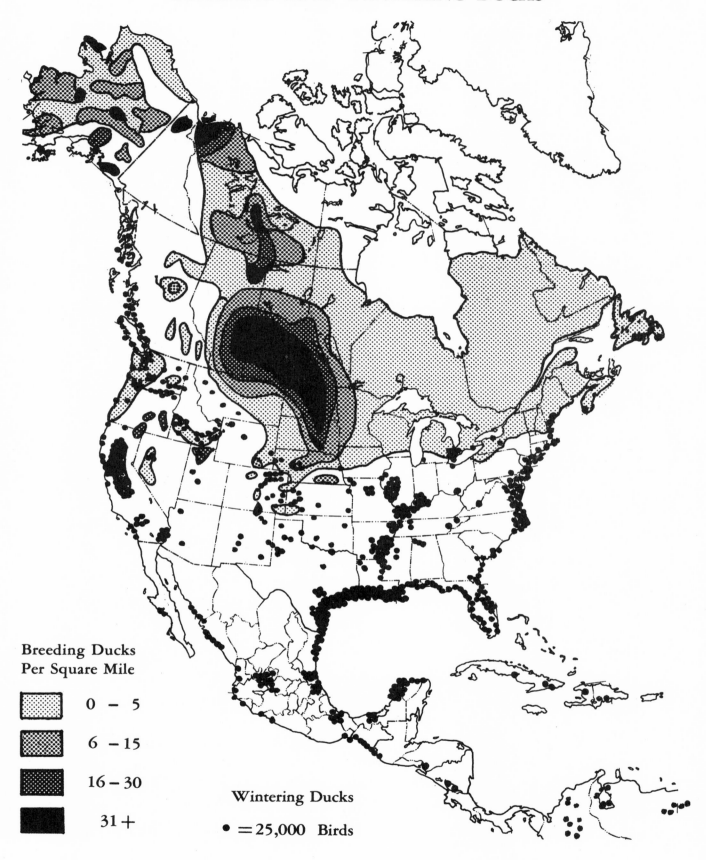

**Breeding Ducks
Per Square Mile**

	0 – 5
	6 – 15
	16 – 30
	31 +

Wintering Ducks

• = 25,000 Birds

begins. They are not always infallible in their judgment on departure dates. Sometimes they leave their winter homes before open water and ample food are available to support them on their way north. Many of these are caught by late storms and wander disconsolately on the frozen ponds and lakes, preferring to risk starvation rather than retreat to a warmer climate.

Most of the waterfowl, however, negotiate their northward trips with an extraordinary good sense of timing. Geese apparently advance north with the isotherm of 35°F., which coincides with the melting of the ice. Long before man was able to fly in his machines, the waterfowl were taking advantage of pressure-pattern navigation.

Many species of waterfowl prefer to remain in their winter resorts until the weather is quite warm in the north. Then they light out and move quickly to their breeding grounds. These fast-flying late migrants may overtake the earlier migrants which have been progressing more slowly north for a month or more, as they followed the retreating ice and snow. Both geese and ducks are daytime migrants, but will also travel at night in clear weather or when pushed for time.

Why do the waterfowl leave their comfortable winter homes and wing their way hundreds or thousands of miles northward, often to unattractive, remote wilderness areas? Why not just stay put and enjoy the more hospitable year-round climate, and avoid all that wearisome travel? There may be at least two plausible reasons why waterfowl find it expedient to go north to nest. First, their winter homes in the south are usually heavily populated with great concentrations of ducks and geese crowding relatively small areas where the water is good and feed abundant throughout the winter months. This crowded condition is hardly conducive to nesting and the proper rearing of young. So the waterfowl, logically, go where there is plenty of open space and elbow room for responsible parents to raise their youngsters under respectable

Nestling in the cattails (Bluewings)
Reproduced by permission of Richard E. Bishop

conditions. A second reason is that in the more remote north country there are fewer predators to prey upon the young. While predators exist in their nesting areas, the waterfowl are scattered rather thinly over millions of acres of breeding ranges, and predators have slimmer pickings than they would if all the ducks were concentrated in smaller areas. Most of the waterfowl must return south to escape the cold. It's also a matter of food supply, which most of the frozen north country does not offer in winter.

All birds have extraordinary stamina to travel the distances they do. No creatures on earth are more athletic. To survive the rigors of the migratory life requires super-Olympic standards of fitness that no human being could possibly equal. Blue geese have been known to make the seventeen-hundred-mile flight from James Bay in Canada to coastal Louisiana in just sixty hours! Many blue-winged teal, banded on their breeding grounds in the north, have covered two to three thousand airline miles in thirty days. Ducks and geese will generally travel from forty to sixty miles an hour, and will fly at these speeds nonstop for hours. Some ducks fly faster than that. A black duck, banded in Ontario, was killed twelve days later in Mississippi, more than one thousand miles away. There are many records of phenomenal flights of waterfowl in migration.

The great wonder of migration is how the birds find their way and return again and again to the same nesting site year after year. Many birds travel at night, and this compounds the mystery, for surely they could not then make use of familiar landmarks. Most waterfowl—geese in particular—seem to follow traditional pathways used over the years by older members of the flocks, who apparently retain a visual memory of all the resting places. These flight routes are seldom in a straight line, but may zigzag and make abrupt turns at different points along the way. Probably the best example of this is the Ross's goose as it migrates southward across the northern Canadian prairies in company with other species of geese. As they approach Great Falls, Montana, the Ross's geese make an abrupt turn westward, leaving their southbound companions, and cross over the Rockies into California. Why do they make that sudden sharp turn at that precise point, year after year? Something tells them that this is the way, and now is the time to turn. Naturalists now believe that the strong homing instinct and navigation, once considered separate functions, are applications of the same faculty.

All the migratory waterfowl species tend to move in the same vaguely established geographical flight patterns. When these

flight lines are plotted on a single map of North America, you see a complex crisscrossing through much of Canada and the northern states. They're flying every which way. But as the birds move southward they begin to separate into four distinct geographic groups called flyways.

The waterfowl specialists say we have two kinds of flyways: biological — the ones established by the waterfowl themselves — and administrative — those determined by people for efficient management and conservation purposes.

The four biological flyways are older than mankind, and they ignore all political boundaries. Each flyway has its own combination of characteristic waterfowl species. However, there is much overlapping and their boundaries can never be defined precisely. They also vary from year to year according to weather conditions. And the flyways reflect the whimsy of living things. The Mississippi flyway, for example, draws birds from clear across the Arctic section of the continent and funnels them into a narrow pathway in the lower Mississippi valley where they spread out eastward and westward along the shores of the Gulf of Mexico. The Atlantic flyway will draw birds from the Yukon Territory, across Canada and down the eastern seaboard.

Some of the secrets of migration are slowly yielding to excellent research around the world, and it gives us better understanding about the travels of waterfowl, where they nest and winter, how they live and die. But the subject of migration is still so muddled and confused by the mass of contradictory evidence and theories that there can be, as yet, no clear, concise answers to this enigma of the bird world. The Creator of the universe, in His infinite wisdom, has obviously provided the birds with all the faculties essential for their successful intercontinental travel. And, knowing neither why nor whence, they respond to compelling forces precisely as He intended they should. This phenomenon, which has confounded men these thousands of years, may well be a realm of natural science which the finite mind of man, with all his ingenious fact-finding, computerized paraphernalia, will not be privileged to fully divine or comprehend. I concur with William Cullen Bryant in his immortal ode, *To a Waterfowl* —

> *There is a Power, whose care*
> *Teaches thy way along that pathless coast, —*
> *The desert and illimitable air,*
> *Lone wandering, but not lost.*

124

On their way (Pintails)

125

THE ATLANTIC FLYWAY

The four major waterfowl flyways may be described as giant funnels into which all of the migrant waterfowl, from all the nesting regions across the continent, pour themselves to eventually arrive at their chosen destinations in both coastal areas, the southern states and points beyond in Mexico and South America. The migrants follow certain definite routes from their widely scattered breeding grounds in the north. Gradually, all of their commonly traveled trails going southward begin to merge in definite geographic regions as they approach their destinations. Thus the long straggling cross-country trails of the countless smaller flocks at last are blended into heavy traffic highways going down into the funnel's tapering throat. On their return journey north, the same lines of flight are followed in reverse, back up the funnel.

The easternmost and most complicated of these funnels is the Atlantic flyway, which encompasses all of the eastern seaboard, west to the Allegheny Mountains, curving northwestward across northern West Virginia and northeastern Ohio to the western end of Lake Erie. Its greatest width is about 500 miles, and it covers 450,000 square miles, or about one-seventh the area of the continental United States.

This flyway is used by the two major groups of ducks, surface-feeders and divers, in about equal numbers. However, of all the ducks taken by hunters in the Atlantic flyway, about 80 percent are the surface-feeding dabblers. And most of these are black ducks, wood ducks, mallards, green-winged teal and widgeon. The black duck is the most abundant.

The greater snow geese and American brant come down this flyway in great numbers from the eastern Arctic and coast of Greenland. This is the same route used by many of the black ducks and Canada geese. Almost all of the black ducks and Canada geese that New England hunters see come from nearby areas, the coastal provinces of eastern Canada, Labrador and Newfoundland. Few, if any, seen in the New England area come from the interior. However, the blacks and Canada geese wintering farther south in the mid-Atlantic states come from interior regions in the far northwest of Canada. This latter route is also the same route used by many of the diving ducks that come down the Atlantic flyway, and others that come southeast across the con-

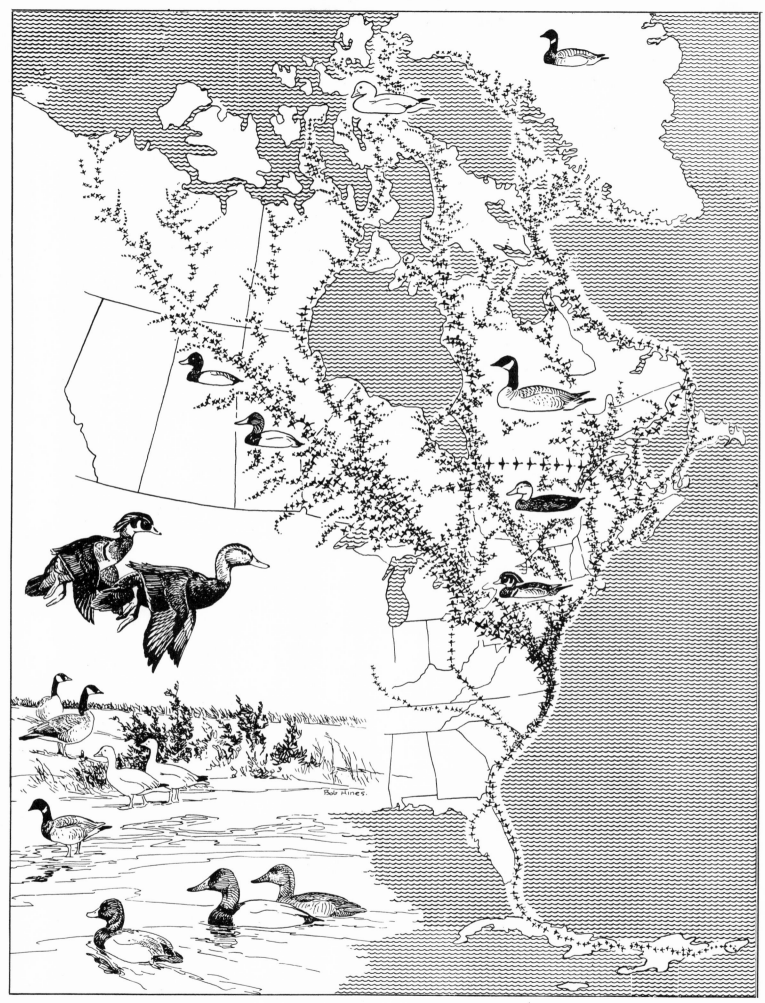

tinent. No diving ducks, except the ringneck, breed in the eastern part of the continent.

Probably the most interesting migration pattern on any of the flyways occurs on the Atlantic with the redhead ducks that breed in the Bear River marshes of Great Salt Lake, Utah. Banding records clearly show that these far western ducks invariably start their fall migration by flying *north* across southeast Idaho, and northwest Wyoming, then swing east across Montana, the Dakotas, Minnesota, Wisconsin and Michigan. Here they join other redheads coming from the north and fly down into the Atlantic flyway to western New York state and along the coast in Maryland and Virginia. This is undoubtedly the most unusual flight pattern of all the waterfowl, as these redheads from Utah actually cross the country at right angles to most of the other major redhead flights going down the Mississippi and Central flyways. There seems to be no explanation for this peculiar behavior, but it does illustrate that ducks have their whims and can be noncomformists, refusing to follow the crowds.

Both species of scaup—lesser and greater—come into the Atlantic flyway. The green-winged teal is quite abundant here, as is the beautiful little wood duck. Almost all species of ducks use the Atlantic flyway, and this gives much of the coastal areas a rich assortment of waterfowl.

Pollution of the waterways has become a serious problem all along this heavily industrialized and populous region, so important to wintering waterfowl. Many watercourses are little better than open sewers. Industrial plants and mines are constantly discharging contaminating chemicals and pollutants into the water systems used by the ducks and geese in this flyway. Oil pollution has also become a serious threat to waterfowl. It is estimated that one hundred thousand ducks and geese are killed annually by oil spillages from ships. The effects of pesticides are becoming increasingly apparent. And the enormous accumulation of spent lead shot from hunters' guns in heavily hunted marshes is a worrisome situation for conservationists. It is significant that there were twice as many ducks wintering in this flyway in the mid-fifties as there were in the early sixties.

The outlook is not entirely pessimistic, however. Much effective work is being done by many agencies and organized groups to improve and reclaim valuable wetland areas in the Atlantic flyway. But it is unlikely that any amount of skillful effort will ever restore this vast waterfowl haven to its original richness.

(continued on page 137)

WINGING SOUTH

Mallards *(Anas p. platyhrynchos)*

129

A QUIET POTHOLE

Pintails *(Anas acuta)*

UNDECIDED

Black Ducks *(Anas rubipres)*

131

TREE HOUSE

Wood Duck, female *(Aix sponsa)*

132

SETTLING DOWN

Green-Winged Teal *(Anas carolinensis)*

133

CHECKING IN

Mallards (*Anas p. platyhrynchos*)

HEADING OUT

Pintails *(Anas acuta)*

NESTLING DOWN

136

Mallards *(Anas p. platyhrynchos)*

THE MISSISSIPPI FLYWAY

The rich, sprawling valley of the Mississippi—the big river, father of waters—is the promised land of milk and honey for the waterfowl. Down through this verdant paradise each fall swarm some eight million ducks, geese, swans and coots, abandoning their northern summer homes to enjoy southern hospitality and the warm winter sun in its southernmost reaches.

The Mississippi flyway offers alluring abundance in massive quantities to all the migrants. It pulls them like a magnet into the vortex of its funnellike form all the way from the Mackenzie River delta and Alaska, Hudson Bay and Baffin Island. In the continental United States this king-size flyway includes fourteen states and 742,000 square miles, one-fourth the area of the forty-eight states. Half of America's waterfowl wetland acreage is contained in this flyway, and here is where hunters take 40 percent of the total duck kill annually.

Because both feed and water all along the way are plentiful and there are no mountains to traverse, long hops for the southbound travelers are not necessary, although some species prefer to make it nonstop all the way. The farmlands and grain fields, the thousands of lakes, and countless prairie potholes, sloughs, and marshes provide all the essentials for the waterfowl traveler, and in the Mississippi flyway they live it up in high fashion.

At least two dozen species of ducks and geese use this flyway regularly. The most dominant route is the long superhighway starting in the Yukon Flats in Alaska, shooting straight down the Mackenzie River, across the great lake and prairie regions of central Canada, and into the United States on a broad front from Montana to Wisconsin. They call it the Mallard Trail, but the pintails, Canada geese, and other species also like to follow this easy road. As the scattered flights roll southward, they begin to converge in a narrow lane along the Mississippi, and from Arkansas on to the Gulf the traffic at peak flight is something to behold!

For all its vastness and outreach across the continent, the Mississippi flyway offers a rather restricted wintering area to all these millions of birds as they concentrate in a thin belt along the Gulf coast and on the inland waters adjacent to the lower Mississippi and its small tributary streams in that area.

Many waterfowl breed within the flyway south of the Canadian

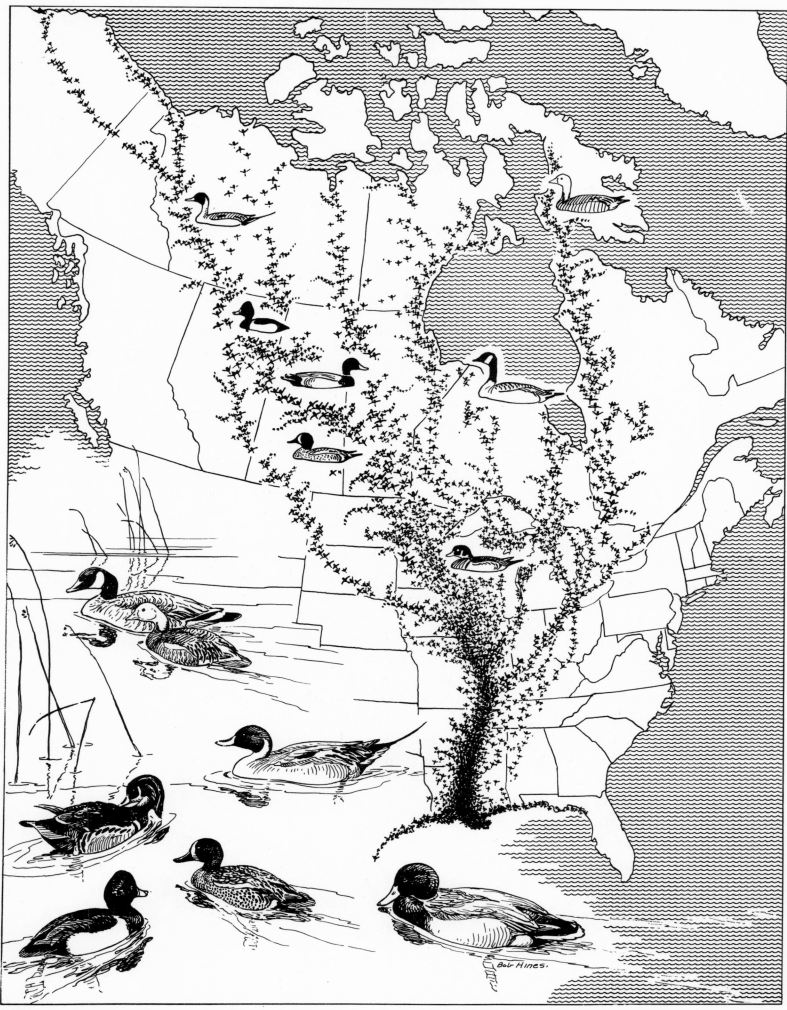

—U.S. Dept. of Interior, Fish and Wildlife Service

border and have but a short trip south. Mallards, pintails, blue-winged teal, black ducks, wood ducks, shovelers, ringnecks, lesser scaup, and some redheads breed in the prairie lands of the north central states. However, the great duck factory, where the major populations nest, is much farther north in the prairies of north central Canada.

Three more or less separate groups of Canada geese come down the Mississippi flyway. The largest contingent comes from west of James Bay. Another comes from Ontario and Manitoba. The smallest group comes from south of James Bay. In 1963, a mid-winter count of the Canada geese wintering in the flyway revealed more than four hundred thousand, the highest on record at that time. Very few white-fronted geese show up in this flyway. The snow geese and blues, however, make a spectacular nonstop flight through the flyway bound for the coastal marshes of Louisiana. In bad weather the snows will abandon their nonstop plans and drop down to rest in unexpected places.

The picture of abundance and well-being in the Mississippi flyway may be misleading, because all is not well. It is true that the flyway is still generous in its offerings to the waterfowl, and a great portion of the legacy remains, but here, as everywhere, man, his industries, and his machines have created great changes and trends that threaten the future of waterfowl. For example, before 1900, Iowa had six million acres of prairie land profusely dotted with potholes, sloughs, and marshes — all ideal duck breeding range. Today only a few dozen marshes remain. This is the story throughout the flyway in the Mississippi valley. Only in Minnesota are there significant chunks of prairie breeding range and this is going fast. Even the far northern breeding grounds in Canada, once thought safe from man's depredation, are becoming more vulnerable as dams and other industrial projects move in to destroy forever this God-given habitat that for centuries has served so ideally as our most productive duck hatcheries.

Will this wonderful Mississippi flyway, home to such great populations of waterfowl, finally fade out in a disastrous finish? Not if you and I and all others who love and cherish our magnificent legacy will learn more about these problems and insist that, at all costs, they be solved. There are answers and solutions. And we have the technical people with the necessary skill and capability. They need our continuing, vigilant support.

MALLARDS
By Bob Hines—
U.S. Dept. of Interior, Fish and Wildlife Service

THE CENTRAL FLYWAY

In the big, wide-open spaces of the prairie country lies the fabulous Central flyway, a continental cornucopia of over a million square miles, one-third of all the flyways put together. Reaching from the Rockies to the Missouri River, this is the expressway over which pass millions of waterfowl moving to and from their nesting areas in the north and their winter homes in Texas, Mexico, and South America.

More than any of the others, the Central flyway is an up-and-downer for ducks, with good years and bad, depending on the available water. The annual rainfall in most of this great plains area is less than twenty inches. A drought means disaster for the ducks, because within this flyway are some of the best breeding grounds. The upper region of the flyway is the great pothole country — Manitoba, Saskatchewan, Alberta, and the Dakotas. When the water is plentiful and the potholes, marshes, and sloughs are full, this is the world's most productive duck factory. But the drought years come all too often, and then the empty ponds are mute evidence that it will be another poor year for ducks all along the flyway. The percentage of good years and prolific hatching seasons, however, is high enough to maintain the Central flyway as the major producer of a variety of species.

The mallard is the choice bird in this flyway and the most numerous of all the dabblers. Pintails, green-winged and blue-winged teal rank next to the mallards. Shovelers, widgeon, and gadwalls are other dabblers quite common on the flyway.

Among the diving ducks, the redheads are most abundant in the Central flyway, and many of these nest in the famous Bear River marshes in Utah, on the border between the Central and Pacific flyways. The canvasback is a northern nester, and many use this flyway in moving down to their wintering grounds on the Texas coast and the east coast of Mexico. Lesser scaup in years past have not been abundant on the flyway, but seem to be on the increase recently, as they come south very late, just ahead of winter. The ringnecks, goldeneyes and other divers are not considered important in this flyway and appear in far less numbers than the other ducks.

Geese like the Central flyway, and it is a popular route for several species. Canada geese, snows, blues, white-fronts, and Ross's all move through this area in great numbers and intermingle as

A quiet haven in flooded timber (Mallards)
Reproduced by permission of Richard E. Bishop

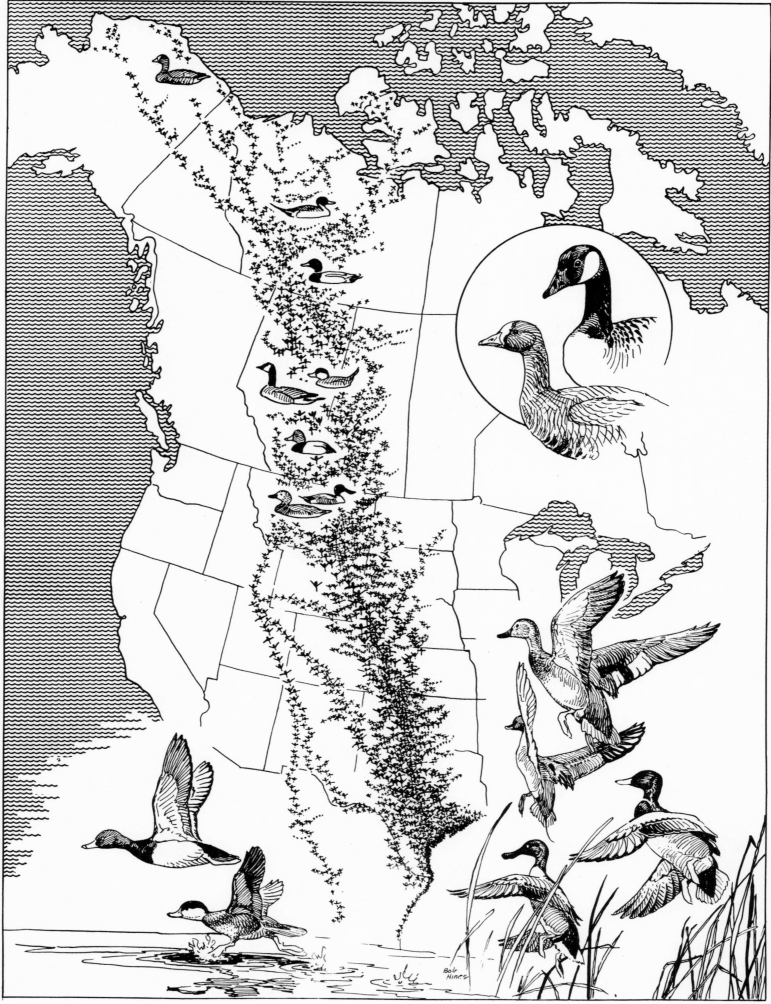

they move north in the spring and south in the fall. Some whistling swans pass over the flyway on their way to and from the Pacific flyway where they winter in California.

The future of the waterfowl in the Central flyway depends on what happens to the water. In the past, drainage and siltation from farmlands has leveled the land and drained precious water from large areas. The scattered pothole and puddle character of this prairie country, however, has proved to be of some advantage for conservation. Since these waters are small and of variable volume, they have not been such attractive projects for the reclamation interests which delight in draining swamps for submarginal and unprofitable agricultural use. Nevertheless, thousands of these potholes in the northern areas of the Central flyway have been drained to make way for agriculture.

On the brighter side, many artificial ponds for waterfowl have been constructed by state and federal conservation agencies, by individuals and conservation groups. Meanwhile, as their habitat has diminished, the ducks and geese somehow adapt to the worsening conditions. They become more dependent on farm crops and fields for feeding, and utilize less favorable nesting conditions.

As the human population grows, competition for land and water will increase accordingly. To save enough to accommodate the waterfowl will be a constant challenge to every conservation-minded citizen.

THE PACIFIC FLYWAY

From the top of the Rockies to the Pacific, from Canada on the north to the Mexican border on the south, the picturesque westernmost states form the waterfowls' Pacific flyway. Seven states, one-fourth of the continental United States—Washington, Oregon, California, Idaho, Nevada, Utah, and Arizona—provide winter homes and a considerable amount of breeding range for many species of ducks and geese as well as swans.

The character of the waterfowl habitat in the Pacific flyway is, for the most part, unlike that of the other flyways. Only one percent of the land west of the Rockies is considered suitable refuge for waterfowl. It is confined to five major units where many species concentrate for wintering, and in lesser numbers for nesting.

The Great Basin—a high intermountain plateau in Nevada and parts of Utah, Oregon, and California—is one important range. Streams and rivers wind through its valleys to gather in shallow lakes. It is arid country, but very productive where water exists in spring and summer. The Bear River marsh lies in this basin and is one of the country's best breeding grounds for redheads, pintails, and cinnamon teal.

The river systems of the Colorado Basin on the western slope of the Rockies, coming down into the lower reaches, form sloughs and marshy habitat that attract waterfowl. The coastal bays and rivers, a third area, along the coast, offer wintering areas, especially for the diving ducks.

The Columbia river system is another wintering and breeding range for limited numbers of ducks and geese. The Sacramento-San Joaquin river drainage basin in California is the largest flatland in this flyway. This well-watered valley is the winter home for a large share of the ducks and geese in the flyway.

The rapid settlement of the West has naturally had a disastrous effect on much of the waterfowl territory. Its character has been greatly altered, even within the last ten years. The increasingly desperate search for water, to supply the mushrooming populations of western cities, and the extensive drainage projects that have flourished make a rather bleak picture for the future of waterfowl in the Pacific flyway.

Mallards are the most common duck in this flyway, with pintails a close second. The mallards come booming down rather late in the season from Alberta, British Columbia, and western Sas-

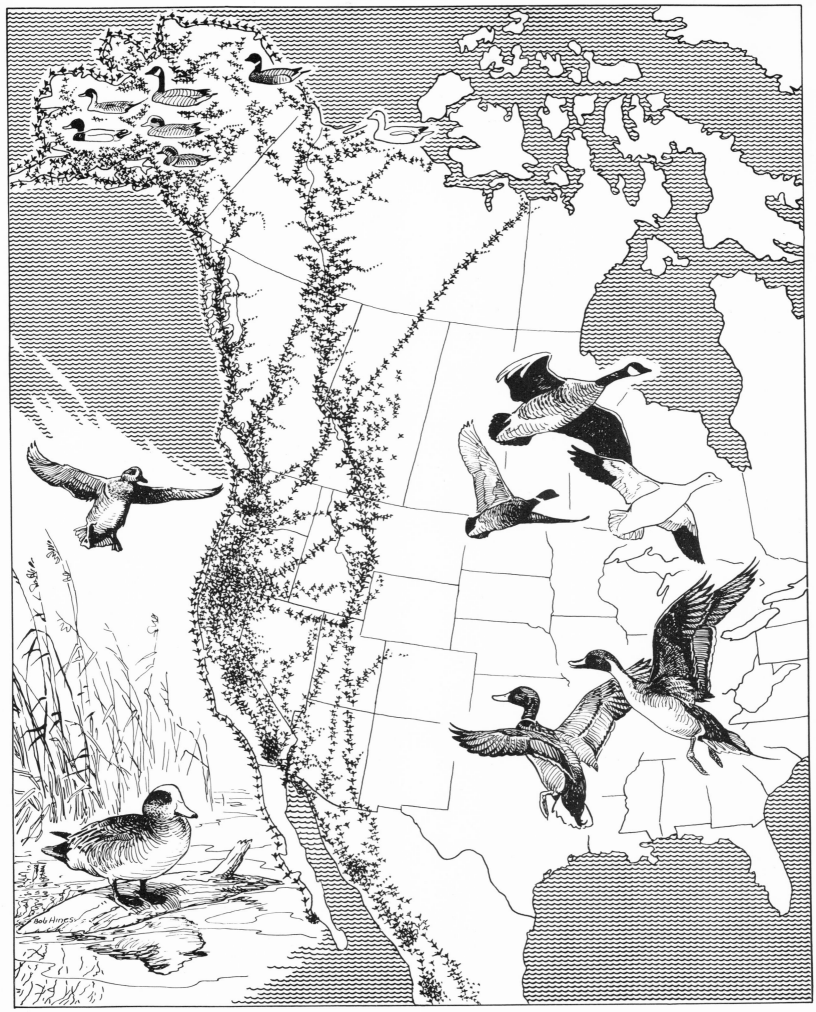

katchewan. Very few of these mallards ever go beyond Los Angeles. The mallards have been helped by the new croplands developed in the irrigated country. They have learned to forage considerable feed from these irrigated crops, since the slough and marsh lands have diminished. This has, understandably, created some tense conflicts with the crop owners, who don't appreciate this wholesale depredation. The solution would seem to lie in providing the ducks with alternate food supplies and feeding areas away from the croplands.

The pintails, once abundant in the Pacific flyway, are no longer one of the most common nesters there, but great numbers, probably about 75 percent of the pintails in the flyway, come into California from Canada to winter.

Widgeon are the third ranking duck in numbers in the Pacific flyway, with gadwalls next. All three species of teal—blue-winged, green-winged and cinnamon—use the flyway, but only the green-wing is abundant. The cinnamon, strictly a western and southern duck, does nest in most of the flyway states, but is neither abundant nor important to the hunter.

The shovelers nest in the northern half of the flyway, and wood ducks nest in the Pacific Northwest and British Columbia. Most of them migrate to the Sacramento-San Joaquin valley to winter.

Of the diving ducks in the flyway, the lesser scaup is the dominant species. Greater scaup, ringnecks, canvasbacks, and redheads are present, but in fewer numbers than the lesser scaup. The ruddy duck is very abundant, and many nest in the Great Basin.

Snow geese, Ross's geese, and cackling geese spend their winters in the Sacramento-San Joaquin valley, migrating from the Arctic regions. The western Canada geese nest within the flyway in the Great Basin and Columbia Basin. Some extend into southern Canada, Montana, Wyoming, and western Colorado. Wintering areas for these Canada geese often include their own nesting areas, except in very severe winters. Black brant come into the flyway from the Arctic tundra and northern Alaska to winter along the coast from Puget Sound to Baja, California.

The whistling swans winter in all the states in the Pacific flyway, but they nest only in the remote tundra of northern Canada and Alaska. They are the latest to come south and the first to leave in the spring. The trumpeter swan, in very limited numbers, is nesting in some ranges in Alaska, Alberta, and along the Continental Divide, near Yellowstone National Park and Red Rock Lakes in Montana.

WHERE DO THEY ALL COME FROM?

As you watch the waterfowl wing southward through the late fall skies, do you ever wonder from what distant nesting places they may have come? Did they come from the nearby potholes, lakes and marshes? Or from the remote reaches of the vast arctic and tundra lands thousands of miles to the north? We can only guess, but their passing high overhead never fails to stir within us a restless urge to capture some of their mystery, their freedom and the blue horizons from whence they came. But we can only stand and watch their speeding forms disappear in the distance, and speculate on their point of origin.

Most of the waterfowl of North America are produced in three major "duck factories:" (1) the prairie, pothole and marsh country; (2) the northern watersheds and deltas; (3) the northern forests and tundras.

In these three nesting regions practically all of our ducks and geese are hatched and reared in the short span of time from May to September.

Prairie Potholes and Marshes

Of the three principal nesting areas, the prairie potholes and marshes are by far the most productive. Although covering only 10 percent of the total waterfowl breeding area on this continent, the potholes and marshes are where 50 percent of the duck crop is hatched in an average year. And more than 50 percent in the good years, when water is plentiful.

This prairie and pothole region, created by advancing and retreating glaciers in the recent Ice Age, covers about three hundred thousand square miles—a strip averaging about three hundred miles wide in south-central Canada and north-central United States—from Edmonton, Alberta; east to Winnipeg; south and southeast across eastern Montana; through the Dakotas and into western Minnesota. When brimming with water, the potholes and marshes are the world's most prolific nesting grounds for ducks. In years of ample snow and rainfall, the prairie country's duck population rockets to staggering numbers. But successive years of drought bring a disastrous decline of ducks in direct proportion

Coming into a quiet bay (Mallards)

to the decline in water, and subsequently tighter hunting regulations.

The pothole country includes flat and rolling and sometimes hilly terrain. Grassland covers the southern two thirds. Wooded areas of fast-growing aspen are taking over the northern third, and this area is now known by game management people as the "parklands." The parklands have somewhat more rainfall and cooler summers which make them more dependable than the drier, warmer southern section for duck production in drought years. Some of the pothole region in northern Montana and southwestern Saskatchewan is still uncultivated virgin prairie, where

148

grazing cattle have replaced the buffalo that once roamed there.

The potholes must have water in them to be of value to ducks. Many do not retain water through the summer, while others are always well watered. There are several types of potholes, and a bit of knowledge about them gives us a better understanding of how they affect the duck population. In *Waterfowl Tomorrow,* published by the U. S. Department of the Interior, the various types of potholes are authoritatively described as follows:

"Sheet-water potholes are shallow depressions, temporarily flooded by melting snows or heavy rains. The water may disappear in a few days, but vegetation in the basin usually is not altered.

"Temporary potholes are covered in spring with as much as 18 inches of water, which usually disappears in 4 to 6 weeks in all but wet years, but often that is enough for plants like rushes, sedges, and cattails. These ponds attract upland nesters and early broods, which must move later in the season to places where there is water.

"Semipermanent or intermediate potholes are basins filled with 2 to 5 feet of water in the spring. Some do not dry out for several years and usually have both aquatic and emergent vegetation. They provide nesting sites for diving ducks and are also used by upland nesting ducks. In terms of broods per unit area, they are the most productive of all types of potholes.

"Permanent potholes may have as much as 10 feet of water. Rushes and water plants may grow in the shallower parts. These potholes often exist in the most recent and least eroded morainal areas of the prairies. Adult ducks often use the larger water areas after nesting when they moult and replace most of their feathers.

"We use the term marsh to describe a large body of water that has irregular shape, completely or partly grown with rushes, sedges, and other emergent vegetation, and frequently with moderate or heavy growths of submerged plants. Prairie lakes are deeper than marshes, may have a band of vegetation along the shoreline, but otherwise are open and windswept."

A major source of pothole water is melting snow and heavy spring rains. If neither is present, the ducks are in trouble. The entire pothole region averages about thirty potholes per square mile in normal years. However, potholes do not occur in nice regular patterns. There can be one hundred or more in a single square mile, but only a half dozen or so in another section nearby. The alarming thing about potholes is their steadily diminishing numbers. Drought years have destroyed many potholes. And farming has changed even more, in both number and location.

Thousands have been drained in Minnesota and eastern North Dakota and South Dakota to create more tillable land. Similar drainage is now starting in some of the pothole regions of Canada.

Fifteen species of ducks commonly nest in the prairie potholes and marshes. Why do these ducks make these risky, unreliable, droughty prairies their chosen nesting grounds? The answer is that they prefer and need the variety, number, and quality of the potholes available. Mallards, teal, and canvasbacks, for example, use several ponds of varied types for mating and nesting. When the breeding season starts, the mated ducks want seclusion for nesting and rearing of young. The number and variety of the potholes can give this needed privacy to a large duck population.

Since all potholes are different, one family of ducks may regularly utilize several potholes in the course of one day. One pothole may have plants that provide escape cover for the young ducklings. Another, perhaps only a few yards away, may provide loafing spots for both adults and young. Another pond nearby may have deep water or a dense growth of submerged vegetation, or an abundance of animal and plant foods. So the ducks move around, using as many nearby ponds as required to fill their routine daily needs. It is possible, of course, that one good pothole could adequately serve all their needs, and this is frequently the case.

Of the fifteen species coming into the pothole and marsh country to nest, the mallard, pintail, and blue-winged teal are the most abundant. The pintails, shovelers, and gadwalls prefer the grasslands. Green-winged teal, lesser scaup, buffleheads, ring-necked ducks, common goldeneyes, and white-winged scoters are more abundant in the parklands, the upper third of the pothole region. Mallards, blue-winged teal, widgeons, redheads, canvasbacks, and ruddy ducks use the entire region indiscriminately. Only rarely do the wood ducks, cinnamon teal, and black ducks nest in either the grasslands or the parklands.

When the adult ducks arrive on the prairie in the spring, most of the ponds and lakes are still frozen. These early birds feed on waste grain in the stubble fields until the water opens up. As the ice goes out, they scatter over the countryside and stake out their summer home sites. By early May, they have settled down to the serious business of raising a family.

The hazards that prairie-bred ducks must cope with are many and fearsome. It is doubtful if human beings could do as well under the same circumstances. Even in good years, nesting ducks that fail to raise a brood far outnumber those that finally succeed. Man with his desire to burn, plow, and drain is a major cause of duck

"Jack pot" (Mallards)
Reproduced by permission of Richard E. Bishop

failure on the prairie. He has not only destroyed desirable wet-lands, but has also polluted much of what remains, or allowed his stock to eat away the vegetation cover so necessary for nesting ducks. On top of this is the long list of wild animals, fish, and birds that prey on ducks and their eggs. Then, those that survive may be stricken with botulism, agal poisoning, parasitic infections, leeches, or killed in one of the severe hail storms that batter the prairie at times. All of these hazards still do not compare in total effect with the damage wrought by drought. There have been years—1959 and 1961 notably—when countless thousands of mated ducks of all species were unable to nest because many of the potholes were dry. But prairie ducks seem born to adversity. In spite of all the discouraging handicaps, they keep coming back from the thin edges of disaster and tenaciously maintain a surprisingly large population year after year.

The Northern Watersheds and Deltas

The most spectacular of North American waterfowl nurseries are the watersheds and deltas of the northern rivers of central and western Canada. The Saskatchewan, Mackenzie, Yukon, Slave and Athabaska rivers all have their origins in the Continental Divide and drain to arctic or subarctic regions. All carry heavy loads of rich silt as they roll along, and this is deposited wherever these rivers reach base level.

The resulting deltas—vast, sprawling and generously watered—are vitally important to the production of waterfowl. They never go dry and their fertile marshes are ideal habitat for many species of ducks and geese. The delta country is especially important when drought hits the prairies to the south and the potholes dry up. Then, many of the prairie ducks move north seeking the well watered deltas where conditions are most like those they are accustomed to. All of the deltas support lush growths of choice duck foods of many varieties, and there is enough to feed millions of hungry ducks with some to spare.

The watersheds and deltas are a relatively small part of the total duck production areas. But they produce a great abundance and variety of ducks and geese. The total delta area is estimated to be about 55,000 square miles. More than a two-million breeding duck population has been estimated on the deltas, and in the years when dried out prairie ducks go north the delta duck population is as high as six million.

On the Saskatchewan delta the lesser scaup is the dominant species, about a third of the total. The blue-winged teal account

(continued on page 161)

THEY'RE COMING IN

Pintails *(Anas acuta)*

153

DAY IS DONE

154

Pintails *(Anas acuta)*

LANDING AREA

Wood Ducks *(Aix sponsa)*

155

STOPPING OVER

Mallards (*Anas p. platyrhynchos*)

CLEARED FOR LANDING

Pintails (*Anas acuta*)

157

SOUTHWARD BOUND

158

Pintails *(Anas acuta)*

EASING DOWN

Gadwalls *(Anas strepera)*

SPREAD FORMATION

Pintails *(Anas acuta)*

(continued from page 152)

for a fifth, followed by the mallards, common goldeneyes, canvasbacks, American widegon, redheads, ruddy, ringneck, shovelers, white-winged scoters, buffleheads, and gadwalls in about that order of abundance. In addition to being a choice nursery area, the Saskatchewan delta, the most southerly of the deltas, is a regular gathering place and rest stop for other thousands of waterfowl during their long treks to and from their more northerly nesting grounds.

The Athabaska delta is the most northerly prairie type, and the ducks found here are much the same species as on the prairies to the south. The mallard is number one here, and the pintail next. Others using the Athabaska delta are canvasback, lesser scaup, shoveler, common goldeneye, redhead, American widgeon, bufflehead, green-winged teal, blue-winged teal, ringneck, gadwall, ruddy, common and red-breasted mergansers and white-winged and surf scoters. And like the Saskatchewan delta, the Athabaska is host to many migrating ducks and geese passing through on their way to and from their breeding areas farther north. It is believed that the entire population of Ross's geese assemble here on their trips between the Arctic coast and California.

The Mackenzie River delta at the Beaufort Sea in the Arctic, supports a duck population ranging from 80,000 to 335,000, depending on the water conditions in the prairie pothole country. In the wooded section the greater scaup is the most abundant species, while in the open, treeless part of the delta the pintail is dominant. Other species nesting here are the American widgeon, white-winged scoter, mallard, common goldeneye, green-winged teal, red-breasted merganser, shoveler and canvasback. Some snow geese occupy the small islands here, and some Canada and white-fronted geese nest here also. Flooding is a serious hazard to nesting ducks on the Mackenzie delta. They have been completely flooded out three times in fifteen years, from 1948 to 1962.

The Yukon River delta at the Bering Sea is the major, if not the only, breeding ground for several species of Pacific flyway waterfowl. Here the cackling geese, black brant, and practically all of the emperor geese nest, as do most of the whistling swans from the western states. Among the ducks, greater scaup and pintail are most abundant, with common scoters, mallards, old squaw and several species of eider ducks all using this nesting area.

There are other smaller deltas in the north country, all similar in general character, each one providing unique habitat appealing to certain species. All of the deltas serve as vast waterfowl reser-

Gliding (Canada Geese)

voirs that are never completely drained and are always capable of maintaining a good breeding-stock nucleus that would doubtless perish if forced to survive the drought years on the prairies. Deltas and the northern watersheds are the major factories for all geese except some Canadas and white-fronts.

The future outlook for the deltas is not a healthy one.

162

Authorities have predicted that the Saskatchewan delta will soon be defunct or seriously damaged by reclamation projects and electric power projects. The Yukon is threatened by dam projects, and oil field development looms as a detriment to the Mackenzie. As one writer on the subject recently said, "we can have kilowatts and canvasbacks—but not from the same place."

Northern Forests and Tundras

Many of our migratory waterfowl do not conform to the general pattern when it comes to choosing nesting grounds. While most species, except geese, prefer the popular pothole country on the prairies or the northern deltas, others of the same species have a preference for the primitive northern woodlands and the harsh, treeless, barren tundra, often described as a land of desolation.

The southern part of the woodland—almost a third of the North American continent—extends from northeastern Minnesota, northern Michigan, northern Pennsylvania, New York and Massachusetts, westward to northern Alberta, British Columbia, and north to Alaska, Victoria and Baffin, and other areas in the Arctic.

The tundra extends from the southern coast of Labrador to Ungava Bay, northwestward from Churchill to north of Great Bear Lake and on to the coast of Alaska near Kotzebue Sound.

The density of waterfowl population in the woodlands and tundra is quite low compared to the concentrations in other types of nesting areas. But the expansive size of the forest and tundra lands, and the countless lakes and streams, make it a useful habitat for many waterfowl species and a substantial contributor to the total population of both geese and ducks. The climate is severe and summers short, but the waterfowl nest here successfully, even in the most northern parts.

One significant asset the forest and tundra country possesses is its stability. It changes very little from year to year, and is never plagued by drought. In drought years on the prairies, the waterfowl produced in these woodland and tundra nesting areas are even more important, and a welcome addition to the diminished crop on the dry prairies.

The interior of the woodland lake country in eastern Canada, the land of the loon, offers nesting grounds in the shallow bays of many lakes for the scaups, mallards, green-winged teal and ring-necked ducks. And more to the east, the black ducks, along with goldeneyes and mergansers find suitable nesting areas. Other species of ducks inhabit various areas in limited numbers.

The interior tundra produces very few ducks, but geese, especially Canada geese, breed over the entire tundra area in scattered groups and pairs. The most attractive waterfowl habitat of the tundra lies along the coastline and coastal plains. Here are very high densities of geese, especially snow geese. All species of geese nest along the coastal tundra, and these areas produce most of the geese of North America. Snow geese are an important food source for the coastal Indians, who take from thirty to forty thousand each year. They save the feathers for stuffing bedrolls and use the rich fat for making bannock.

The stable character of these vast woodland and tundra areas may, in the future, prove to be of even greater importance to the survival of our waterfowl. It is unlikely that man, for all his greed and destructive qualities, will exert any great adverse influence on these remote regions as habitat for waterfowl. It is reasonable to believe that this north country will continue to be a dependable summer refuge for breeding waterfowl, and could be a major factor in the preservation of ducks and geese, if and when habitat elsewhere is eventually destroyed.

LATE ARRIVALS (MALLARDS)
By Bob Hines—U.S. Dept. of Interior, Fish and Wildlife Service

MALLARD HEAVEN IN THE PIN OAK FLATS

Deep in the throat of the Mississippi flyway funnel lies the Grand Prairie of Arkansas, some of the first land to come under the hand of the white man, and the last to feel the blade of his plow. Nestling between the foothills of the Ozarks on the west and the narrow strip of hills on the east known as Crowley's Ridge, the Grand Prairie reaches south until its apex merges into the flood plain below Arkansas Post, where the Arkansas River joins the Mississippi.

On this broad plain are the pin oak flats and rice fields that have made such towns as Stuttgart and DeWitt famous as the duck capitals of the world. No duck could ask for a more abundant life than that provided by thousands of acres of juicy acorns and delicious rice, combined with ample water and a friendly winter climate. In Arkansas the ducks have it made. No wonder they pour into this heavenly winter haven by the millions, winging down from all points north—the bleak tundra, the barren wastes of the upper Yukon, the Manitoba prairies, and the sprawling deltas of the great Canadian watersheds. Many are content to remain here through the winter, lolling in the lazy well fed life that the Grand Prairie offers. Others, passing through, linger to live it up for a few days before moving to other winter resorts southward.

How long the ducks have enjoyed this acorn bonanza no one knows. Perhaps for centuries. But like every utopia, this one has had a slight hitch in it. Water! The success of the pin oak flats as a duck refuge from year to year has depended entirely upon the fall and winter rains soaking the ground and pushing the numerous creeks and rivers out of their banks to flood the extensive hardwood bottomlands. Then, and only then, could the ducks use this rich feeding paradise. There must be flood water under the oaks and other nut trees that abound in this area. Some years the rains fail to come, or are too little or too late. Then the disappointed ducks, finding no water, go elsewhere to feed. And this is disaster for the Grand Prairie people, as well as for the ducks. Many communities in the Grand Prairie have an important economic stake in the duck hunting season that draws the country's best hunters for the fabulous shooting. This is the up-and-down situation that prevailed until the ingenious duck hunters of the Grand Prairie came up with an idea for improving on nature, an idea that would guarantee the ducks the water they need, and the hunters all the ducks they could legally take.

The great idea originated in the Stuttgart area. The plan was to flood the pin oak flats artificially and keep the ducks coming in on schedule. It worked beautifully! The hardpan underlying the soil holds water like a saucer, just as it does on the nearby irrigated rice fields. Now, every fall the oak flats are systematically and carefully flooded in October, just as the leaves are turning color. The trees still look green, but dormancy has actually set in, and the flooding does them no harm. The water, from one to eighteen inches deep, remains under the trees throughout the winter, and is drained off in February after most of the ducks have begun to move north. Now the pin oak flats are known as "green tree reservoirs."

The Grand Prairie produces more than a fifth of the nation's rice crop in irrigated fields. By November, when the ducks arrive, the rice has been harvested, but the dry stubble fields are strewn with rice kernels shattered off during the harvest. The rice is by no means wasted. This is what provides a bountiful food supply for the millions of migrants that inhabit the Grand Prairie through the winter months. At night the ducks feed in the rice fields, returning by day to the placid, dark, wooded waters of the pin oak flats. Here, under the colorful fall foliage, they happily divide their time between drowsing, preening, and dipping down for the succulent acorns that carpet the forest floor. It would be difficult to imagine a more idyllic life for ducks. Nothing to interfere with their daily schedule of loafing, sleeping, eating, and luxuriating in the warm sun. But consider the hazardous existence the ducks endure as they journey to and from their distant nesting grounds twice yearly, and the ceaseless struggle they must wage against many enemies and natural dangers as they attempt to rear their families.

In the face of these odds, the ducks are well deserving of this short interval of peace and plenty. This is the way they were intended to live. There should be many more heavenly havens like this.

For a few years, the green tree reservoir idea was an exclusive product of eastern Arkansas and continued to support Stuttgart's claim as the mallard capitol of the world. But the word got around and by the mid fifties other green tree reservoirs were

Along the bayou (Mallards)
Reproduced by permission of Richard E. Bishop

in operation in a number of states in the lower Mississippi valley, where forests of nut producing trees were abundant, and the soil could retain the flood water. By 1963, most states in the lower Mississippi flyway had successful green tree reservoirs going. And several states in the Atlantic picked up the idea and put similar projects into operation. The success of these artificially produced refuges can be illustrated by the example of the Noxubee National Wildlife Refuge, near Starkville, Missouri. Once considered of rather minor importance to ducks, with a peak duck population of 21,000, after a 400-acre green tree reservoir was established, the number rose quickly to 46,000. A second green tree reservoir of 340 acres at Noxubee has now pushed the peak duck population there to well over 100,000 during the winter months.

In the Stuttgart area, it is common to see 50,000 mallards occupying a 100-acre tract of pin oak flats. And as many as 250,000 ducks may be temporarily concentrated on a few hundred acres. In the better years, Fish and Wildlife Service officials have counted a million ducks on a 1600-acre flat. When both the artificially developed areas and the natural over-flow bottoms are well watered by man and nature, the pin oak flats of Arkansas probably contain the bulk of the mallards that come down the Mississippi flyway.

Mallards are by far the predominant species using the Arkansas pin oak flats, estimated to be 90 percent of the total ducks in that area. The other 10 percent are mostly wood ducks who find this habitat to their liking since trees are very much a part of their life. However, just about all of the dabbler ducks are represented in these green tree reservoirs as well as limited numbers of diving ducks, such as ringnecks, lesser scaup, and redheads.

Lucky is the hunter who can enjoy the sporty shooting that this pin oak country affords. It is fast and difficult shooting. Shooting can be done from blinds rigged over the shallow water under the trees, but the real fun shooting is done simply by standing knee-deep in water beside a tree trunk, and pulling the mallards down with an enticing call, without benefit of decoys. As the big greenheads come pitching in over the treetops, they appear to be easy targets. But many a hot shot has found he needs a second box of shells before connecting with his limit.

A bonus that comes free to the hunter and bird watchers who visit the pin oak flats in November is the delightful combination of shirtsleeve weather and the riotous color of the fall foliage. The gold and crimson leaves of the hickory, pin oak, and sweet gum trees form a spectacular canopy that is brilliantly mirrored in the dark-stained water below. Against this picture book backdrop, the hunter waits in the early morning sun for the mallards to return from their feeding in the rice fields. It's a comfortable and enviable setting compared to the frigid, windbitten struggle that northern hunters must undergo for a brief look down the gun barrel at a couple of ducks racing for dear life from the bombardment of a dozen other hunters surrounding a small cow pasture slough.

In they come (Mallards)

SMOOTH LANDING (SNOW GEESE)
By Bob Hines—U.S. Dept. of Interior, Fish and Wildlife Service

HERE COME THE GEESE!

As winter retreats from the great Mississippi flyway and the last remnants of ice disappear from the lakes, potholes and marshes, one of nature's most spectacular dramas begins its annual production in the prairie country of the Dakotas.

When the curtain rises on this unique pageant of the potholes, a small but enthusiastic audience of faithful patrons, bundled in warm clothes, assembles to witness again, as they have for years, the multitudes of wild geese moving in clamoring hordes northward to summer homes in the far regions of the north country.

I have had the good fortune to occupy a box seat on several occasions to view this superb spectacle, and I am convinced that in all our natural world there is no event that can compare in magnitude with the thrilling and awesome sight of thousands of wild geese, solidly blanketing a marsh, and the startling thunder of their beating wings as, in sudden fright, they rise like a giant carpet.

It is usually early April when the first word comes from the local game wardens in South Dakota that the geese have arrived. Those are stirring words! They are the signal to quickly abandon the city and all its irksome responsibilities, to pack the hip boots, wool shirts, parkas, and binoculars, and head for South Dakota. To the seasoned observer of the goose migration, nothing short of death could detain him from joining in the annual welcome to those beautiful voyageurs of the sky who play the starring roles in this enthralling drama.

For several weeks, countless thousands of Canada geese, snows and blues, using the eastern prairie sections of the Mississippi flyway, work their way leisurely north from their winter homes in central Missouri, Louisiana, and Texas. They loaf along the river sand bars and open water, keeping just behind the receding ice, and foraging for whatever waste grain and other feed is available in nearby fields. As the smaller flocks move along, they join others until great concentrations are forming along the Missouri river bottoms. When at last a few warm days leave the potholes and marshes of eastern South Dakota free of ice, the advance troops come wheeling in with a great clamor. In a day or so, the whole host of them roars into the prairies like a snowstorm.

From the very day they depart their winter quarters, these precious flocks are under the constant surveillance of special patrols of federal and state game wardens, whose duty it is to protect the migrants from poachers and any other dangers that may threaten them on their long journey. These radio-equipped patrols maintain a continuous lookout, and from hour to hour they know the exact location of each flock. As the geese move north, the wardens follow and continue the guard duty all through the spring migration until the major concentrations have safely crossed the Canadian border and are well on their way to their chosen nesting sites far to the north.

Some years the migration is more impressive than others. If the weather is bad, the spring late, or extremely hot weather hastens the season, the geese either cut short their stay or sail over with hardly a stop. Then the big show on the prairies can be disappointing.

My first experience with this fascinating event was near DeSmet, South Dakota, in company with my good friend, Wally Gustafson, a great duck hunter and photographer who had discovered the joy and excitement of shooting these beautiful migrating birds with his cameras and telephoto lens. With his 35mm camera and long lens mounted on a gun stock, Wally had been getting some prize-winning pictures of both geese and ducks on his annual pilgrimage to the Dakota migration scene. I became imbued with his enthusiasm and spent several weekends during the winter fashioning a gun stock mount for my camera and 400mm telephoto lens. When, in early April, the game warden in DeSmet called to inform Wally that the flight was in, we were off that very night, bound for goose country.

I shall never forget the memorable days of that first adventure with the geese on the Dakota prairies. Fortunately, it was one of the better seasons. The geese were there by the tens of thousands and in no hurry to leave. The warden spotted us one sunny morning on a large slough which he said contained the greatest concentration of geese in that area—probably twenty-five thousand Canadas, snows and blues. When we arrived, the geese had already returned to the slough from their morning feeding in the stubble and corn fields. I could hardly believe what I saw. Every inch of that slough seemed covered with geese! They were packed in so tightly that hardly a glimmer of water was visible. "Just get settled somewhere," the warden said, "and you'll take a lot of good pictures. These geese will stay here until midafternoon; then they'll take off for their evening feed."

We carefully worked our way around the slough and positioned ourselves in a strategic place, where we could command a good view of the entire area. We were within fifty feet of the shore and hidden only by rather sparse vegetation. But since the geese had not been alarmed, we set up the cameras and began shooting the occasional small groups that kept flying in and out. Some came in just over our heads, so close that it was difficult to focus the cameras on them or swing the gun stock mounts to keep them in the sights. The grand mixture of Canada geese, snows and blues—all seemingly enjoying each other's company—was an interesting display of togetherness. It reminded me of the beach at Coney Island packed with Sunday afternoon bathers and picnickers.

Then we had an unexpected bonus. The ducks began stealing the show. One end of the slough was filled with rushes and other vegetation that apparently concealed some ducks. Our first surprise came when a great flock of big mallards clattered up out of the rushes and headed for the fields. The geese sat tight. Soon, another large flock of mallards zoomed out of concealment and roared off. Every twenty to thirty minutes another flock of a hundred or more mallards churned up out of that rush-grown end of the slough. They kept coming out that way all morning. It was difficult to believe that the relatively small area could hold so many ducks with not a single one visible. We estimated that five thousand mallards had been hiding in that slough when we arrived.

It was a perfect day for our mission—warm and sunny, without a trace of wind, which is usually a part of every South Dakota day. The thousands of geese spread out before us seemed perfectly content. With their gizzards full, there was nothing to do but doze in the sun, preen feathers, or gabble softly to each other. For so many noisy geese, they were surprisingly quiet.

After an hour or so, some snows and blues began moving in close to shore very near where we sat. There was no doubt that they could see us through the thin cover, but they paid no heed. Toward noon, we risked moving from behind the cover and crawled slowly into the open, nearer shore. Still, the geese did not spook. Encouraged by their unconcern, we sat up in plain sight and began shooting pictures. Instead of lighting out, the ones near us moved still closer to look us over. They were all blues and snows. The Canadas kept to the other side of the slough. The curious ones moved to within a dozen yards of us, and I would estimate that at one time a hundred or more snow and blue geese were literally staring down our telephoto lens. They talked back

Caught napping (Mallards)

173

and forth, discussing the situation. Apparently deciding we were harmless, they resumed their dozing, preening, and poking around in the shallows for whatever stray tidbits of food they could uncover.

As the afternoon wore on, we could sense their growing restlessness. It would soon be their feeding time, and they were feeling the hunger pangs. We wanted to be prepared for that moment when they took off. We knew it would be the climactic finish to this rewarding day. With cameras fully loaded, lenses checked and double checked, we waited expectantly. The gabbling grew louder and more insistent as the leaders alerted their groups that the hour of departure was approaching. Then, as if by some prearranged signal, the slough seemed to lift like a flopping blanket. Thousands of clattering wings roared off the water like a clap of thunder. Their shrill cries stabbed at our eardrums. It was deafening, tumultuous, brain-jarring pandemonium that so overwhelmed us we could scarcely lift the cameras to shoot the spectacle. The sun was suddenly blotted out with clouds of screaming bodies, milling in massive confusion. Finally, we recovered enough to start working the cameras. The whirling maelstrom drifted off, and soon flocks were breaking out to go their way toward favorite fields. In moments they were gone, only their faint cries drifting back on the quiet afternoon air. Now the slough was empty. The silence was stunning. But we had the pictures we had come for. And we knew we had witnessed a tremendous exhibition that few people ever see—one of the dramatic productions in this mad modern world that could be recommended as good family entertainment.

LONG-LEGGED WADERS AND SHORE BIRDS

The herons, storks, and ibises are grouped under the order of *Herodiones* and families of *Plataleidae, Ibididae,* and *Ciconiidae.* These are the long-legged wading birds we see along the shore lines and shallow muddy flats. Their necks are long and easily curved into sharp S-shapes. Their wings are rounded, long, and broad. Tails are short and heads usually are naked. In this interesting group, we will briefly relate the characteristics of the roseate spoonbill, white ibis, and American egret.

The snipes and sandpipers are, under the order of *Limicolae,* and the *Scolopacidae* family. The group includes a large number of species all closely allied, generally small or medium sized, short-legged waders. Most species are quite plain and inconspicuous in coloration. Bills are usually long, soft-skinned, straight, roundish, and slim, but on some species they curve up or down. The head is feathered to the bill. Wings are long, flat, and pointed.

The Roseate Spoonbill

Hardly more than twenty years ago the resplendent pink-and-white roseate spoonbill *(Ajaia ajaja)* of the Florida Keys and Texas Gulf were practically extinct. But in the past two decades, thanks to the National Audubon Society and an enlightened public, the spoonbills have made a remarkable comeback. Years ago they were virtually wiped out by the plume hunters and thoughtless vandals who shot them and maliciously destroyed their nests.

The spoonbill population today is far from thriving. Although pitifully small, in total numbers, the spoonbill is in no immediate danger of complete disappearance. Authorities estimate there are no more than fourteen hundred nesting pairs in the United States. However, the encroaching real estate developments on the Florida Keys have been decreasing the spoonbill population, and unless all the remaining nesting and feeding areas that spoonbills require are permanently set aside, their future is definitely uncertain.

If you are a Florida visitor and see some spoonbills, don't label yourself as an outlander by calling them flamingos, as so many tourists do. The spoonbill is a radiantly beautiful creature with its pink-and-white plumage, set off with startling patches of carmine, saffron, and orange yellow. Its rich coloration more than compensates for the unglamorous bare head and odd spoon-shaped bill. Both the male and female are identical in appearance.

The roseate spoonbill, the largest North American member of the ibis family, is essentially a bird of the tropics. The Florida colonies winter in the West Indies, while the Gulf colonies winter in Mexico. There are six distinct spoonbill species in the world, but our New World species is the only brightly colored one. The others are native to Europe, Africa, Asia, and Australia and are all white.

In Florida, spoonbills nest in the mangrove islands in Florida bay. They start building their platforms of sticks in the trees in November. Both male and female share in the three-week task of incubating the two, three, or four eggs. Their pink-and-white powder puff chicks are hatched just before Christmas, completely helpless, fragile looking and seemingly too weak to survive. But their appearance is deceiving. The babies thrive and grow rapidly under the constant, protective care of both parents. By late January they are out of the nest, ready to try their wings. The Gulf coast spoonbill colonies find refuge in the Vingtune Islands and other islands of Galveston Bay, where they are under the watchful eye of the National Audubon Society.

The bird's broad spoon-shaped mandibles—quite rare among birds—are very efficient for food gathering. It wades along shore, swinging its partly opened bill from side to side in a 180-degree arc, feeling for its food through a curtain of water and mud. Spoonbills eat a great variety of food: killifish and other small fry, crustaceans, larvae, water insects, and some vegetation. Great numbers of these small animals are required to make a meal for two or three voracious youngsters in the nest.

For the most part spoonbills are silent, although when feeding and tending the nests they utter a low croaking sound. As do all birds, the spoonbills have natural enemies that constantly plague them during the nesting season. Peregrin falcons, fish crows, grackles, and raccoons are some of the most troublesome marauders that take a toll of eggs and young. Hurricanes, drought, and unseasonable cold spells are always a threat to the spoonbills' survival. But the chief enemy is still man himself.

The spoonbill in flight presents a pretty picture. The long ex-

(continued on page 185)

IN THE VERDANT WOODS

Ruffed Grouse *(Bonasa umbellus)*

177

BLASTING OFF

178

Ruffed Grouse *(Bonasa umbellus)*

PRAIRIE DWELLERS

Prairie Chicken (*Tympanachus cupido pinnatus*)

179

BREAKING COVER

Ring-Necked Pheasant *(Phasianus colchicus torquatus)*

TIME TO SCATTER

Bobwhite quail *(Colinus virginiana)*

181

FLUSHED

Bobwhite quail *(Colinus virginiana)*

HILL-TOPPERS

Red Grouse

183

STARTLED GOBBLERS

184

Wild Turkey *(Meleagris gallapavo silvestris)*

(continued from page 176)

tended bill and neck, huge wing spread, and long red feet extended far beyond the tail give them a streamlined appearance resembling a colorful aircraft. Most ibises flap, sail, then flap again; the spoonbill usually just keeps flapping along at a steady pace. They fly in V's and sometimes in nicely ranked echelons. To visitors in Florida, their pink pinions flashing in the setting sun are a lovely sight as their long diagonal lines return from their feeding grounds.

The people of Florida, Texas, and Louisiana are proud of their roseate spoonbills. Hopefully, they will continue to guard them and maintain the remaining nesting areas to insure the survival of these splendid creatures.

White Ibis

Nothing can truly equal the sight of wild geese passing high overhead, but they do have a close competitor in the white ibis *(Eudocimus albus)*. Few sights in the bird world are as thrilling as the long ribbons of white ibis sailing serenely over the Everglades of Florida or across a marsh anywhere in the low country of the deep South. As they come streaming home by the thousands from their feeding late in the day, in flocks and long weaving lines, their pure white plumage and black tipped wing feathers flashing in the sun, they create a spectacular panorama that one does not soon forget. Flap—sail—flap, they come in low but swiftly. Their peculiar flight habit of alternately flapping, sailing, flapping is a characteristic of most species of ibis. As the advance ranks draw near, they swoop up above the trees, then plummet down into the rookery like a storm of white paper. Now we can see they are medium sized, about 24-inch body length, all white, with wings tipped in blue-black, and bright red legs and bill, the long bill curving downward.

They throng into the rookery until every tree and bush seems buried under blobs of fresh snow. Their bulky nests of twigs and leaves are crowded among the trees and bushes over the shallow water. And we notice that herons and egrets have claimed a share of the rookery with their nests established alongside the ibis.

The white ibis (often called Spanish curlew or white curlew, although it is no relation to the curlew) ranges along the coastal areas from Baja, California, and South Carolina, south to northern South America and the West Indies. Occasional wanderers are seen as far north as in Illinois, South Dakota, and New England, but these are probably immature birds satisfying their wanderlust before settling down in the crowded rookeries.

The white ibis is a sociable bird, content to live in jam-packed rookeries where nesting pairs share all the responsibilities of rearing three or four youngsters. The older ibis prowl the nearby tidal waters or marshes for frogs, small fish, snails, and young water snakes. They pursue their quarry on their long stiltlike legs and probe with the long slender mandibles. With thousands of these hungry waders congregated in such heavy concentrations, one can imagine the enormous amount of food and feeding range the ibis require.

The fish crows and grackles annoy the ibis constantly and destroy many eggs, forcing the ibis to continue laying eggs in an effort to produce a hatch.

Common Egret

One summer evening years ago while fly fishing along a small stream in southern Minnesota, I waded quietly around a bend and saw just ahead of me a beautiful, pure-white, heronlike bird, with long black legs. It stood in the shallows near shore, intently watching the water. I was accustomed to disturbing the great blue herons that fished along the stream, but what was this strange and exotic bird that was slightly smaller than the blue heron? Silently it flapped up over the trees and disappeared. I watched its graceful wings. It was a magnificent bird. Then I remembered that the common egret, or American egret (*Casmerodius albus egretta*), frequently wandered north, far from its usual range in the south. The long, black, wading legs, the sharp, yellow bill and the snow white plumage, with delicate aigrette plumes along the back, were sure evidence that this was indeed the common egret. The first I had seen in the wild state.

Since then I have seen the common egret many times in Minnesota, stalking sedately along small streams and lakeshores, fishing in the familiar manner of all the herons. The ornithologists say that once the young of the egret are on their own, many of the old birds wander north during the summer as far as the Canadian border. In recent years I have seen several of these lonely wanderers boldly fishing the shores of the lake near my home in

Lush plumage (Egret)

the heart of the city. In spite of their snowy white plumage, they remain inconspicuous as they stand upright and rigid waiting for fish to move within range. Few people ever see or recognize them.

The egrets are colony-nesters, breeding in central and tropical North America. In the United States they range from the cypresses of South Carolina to the mangroves of Florida, from the willows of Texas to the tules of Oregon.

At the height of the nesting season the egret's rookery is a very busy and crowded place, with its hundreds of nests jammed into the trees and bushes. The scene is always a confusion of birds coming and going, flapping and quarreling. And, like most warm-climate rookeries, the stench is insufferable. Hatching and rearing a family in this ghettolike atmosphere is wearisome drudgery that both mom and pop nevertheless cheerfully share. They alternate at brooding the eggs, and, to break the dull routine, often make this changing of the guard a rather impressive ceremony. Perhaps the strain of these parental duties under the trying conditions of the rookery is why more of the oldsters these days are wandering far off by themselves, once the youngsters have left home. They just want to get away from it all and be alone for a few blessed summer weeks in the cool north country. Who would deny these faithful parents these well-earned pleasures?

All of the adult egrets in the rookery are off to the feeding grounds at sunrise. With their lancelike bill they make short work of collecting fish, snakes, mice, insects, and frogs. Then back to the rookery to feed the three or four hungry nestlings impatiently waiting with outstretched necks and gaping mouths. The parent makes contact and regurgitates a portion of the catch into the stomach of each young one. They are fed at least four times daily. On this schedule they grow rapidly and in a few weeks are perching on the nearest tree limb, ready to fly up and away into the big, wide, wonderful world spread out before them.

The elegant beauty of the egret, with its lovely nuptial plumes, called aigrettes, was its curse in the early 1900's. Up to fifty-four of these snowy back feathers form the egret's nuptial train. The milliners at one time were paying as much as thirty-two dollars an ounce for these egret plumes to adorn their customers' hats. The egret hunters went wild and in their greed came very near annihilating the egret. Had it not been for the intervention of the National Audubon Society and the establishment of sanctuaries, we would almost certainly have no egrets today. Now, because the egrets have nesting range and protection, they have revived and are on the increase.

Wilson's Snipe

Almost any boy who has attended a summer camp can tell you about "snipe hunting" the way campers do it. When I was a boy, it was a hallowed tradition to initiate the young first-year campers with an after-dark snipe hunt. The novices, each supplied with a gunny sack, were taken into the woods, spotted in a lonely remote place, and told to wait there quietly with the gunny sacks held open on the ground. The idea was for the rest of us smart alecks to go out and chase the snipe toward the open sacks. If the sack holders were quiet the snipe would run into the bags. We would then depart, go back to camp, and crawl into bed, leaving the unsuspecting snipe hunters literally holding the bag, while they fought mosquitoes and tried not to scare off the snipe. Eventually, they would realize they had been taken in and would come dragging sleepily back to camp, consoled by the fact that they had now been duly initiated.

But real snipe hunting is nothing like that. It is an exciting and challenging sport, and this little game bird is full of tricks that baffle even the most experienced shooter.

The Wilson's snipe—also called common snipe and jack-snipe—resembles the woodcock in both appearance and in some of its habits. It has a long bill, similar to the woodcock, and uses it to probe for worms and food in soft ooze in the marshes. But it does not bore with it in the solid earth, as the woodcock does. Unlike the woodcock, the snipe prefers the open country rather than the wooded areas. It likes the low, wet, swampy meadows and ponds, where it hunts for its food in the shallow water and oozy mud. Snipes are daylight feeders, consuming snails, small crustaceans, and aquatic insects, in addition to worms.

Like the woodcock and many other shore birds, the Wilson's snipe has a flight song of unusual quality. It may be heard mornings and evenings during the mating and nesting season. The bird rises swiftly to a height of perhaps 150 feet above its home in the meadow and circles round and round on rapidly vibrating wings, dipping and rising erratically. As it dives, the rush of air through the outer feathers of its spread tail produces strange, low-pitched, pulsating notes that are one of nature's most eerie sounds. This is the mating song of the Wilson's snipe.

When you first hear the snipe song you scan upward trying to locate its source. You see nothing at first, and the sound seems to come from nowhere in particular. Then you make out the tiny,

high-circling speck, gyrating like a Turkish dancer.

When flushed from its cover in the marsh or meadow, the snipe complains in a harsh, raspy voice that sounds like *scaap, scaap.* Off it darts, twisting and skidding as it rockets up into the air. You have to be a sharpshooter to bag these deceptive little fellows, and that's what makes snipe hunting a fun sport.

The snipe nest on the ground, usually near water, hiding the grass-lined nest among the ferns, sedges or rushes. Four olive-brown eggs are the usual clutch.

We find Wilson's snipe just about everywhere in the United States except California, Nevada, and New Mexico. It also ranges through southern Canada from the Atlantic coast to northern Manitoba. The northern snipe migrate in the winter to the Gulf region and other southern states.

Feathery grace (Herring Gulls)

WATERFOWL DO THE STRANGEST THINGS!

Waterfowl can be a delightful source of entertainment for anyone willing to sit patiently and watch the show. Ducks and geese have a capacity for many strange, comical, even hair-raising performances in the air and on the water. Ducks, in particular, possess an impressive talent for unusual behavior, and to those who observe them closely, their repertoire of stunts and tricks seems endless.

Have you ever seen a duck flying upside down? Or backwards? Or doing a loop-the-loop? You may say that ducks never do that, but the slow-motion movie camera has proved many times that ducks perform all of these astonishing feats. Richard E. Bishop, whose wildfowl pictures are featured in this volume, has filmed considerable footage of ducks flying in the most extraordinary attitudes — upside down, backwards, looping-the-loop — and executing other dazzling feats that equal or exceed the ability of the best aircraft stunt fliers.

When necessary, a duck can perform any imaginable aerial maneuver, doing it more quickly and with more grace than a stunt flier would, and always pulling out of it a whole duck, with both wings securely attached. All of these remarkable actions are completed so quickly that they cannot be detected by the unaided human eye. Hunters occasionally see a duck, suddenly frightened, instantly reverse its course while in full flight. This may sound impossible, but the slow-motion camera reveals how it is done. The duck does what fighter pilots call the Immelmann turn. The bird does a half loop over and flies a few wing beats on its back, wings over, and rights itself as it reverses course. Such trickery baffles the hunter. His eye cannot follow what actually happens. But it's a neat way for a duck to escape sudden death.

Sometimes ducks pull a boo-boo while landing or taking off. They misjudge the wind, their speed, or become careless with their technique and lose their balance. When this happens, a duck coming into the water may flop over and hit the water upside down, or roll over and plop under water. When suddenly alarmed, a duck may fly out of the water so rapidly it will lose its balance and actually fly backwards before recovering. Air pockets are a

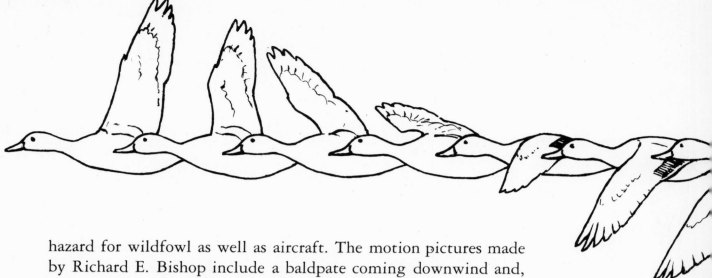

hazard for wildfowl as well as aircraft. The motion pictures made by Richard E. Bishop include a baldpate coming downwind and, while making a sharp turn to land, falling helplessly down through an air pocket several feet deep, and hitting the water with a terrific splash.

All of these incredible deeds are a rather routine part of ducks' very existence, but it is difficult to convince the skeptics that ducks actually do these strange things until they see the irrefutable evidence in a slow-motion film.

Most ducks are smart and wary. They have to be these days to survive the hundreds of thousands of hunters waiting for them on every likely pond and lake. Ducks have learned to exercise great caution in choosing their feeding and resting stops during migration. But ducks and other waterfowl, like human beings, are unpredictable at times, and, on occasions, even the smartest ducks are guilty of sheer stupidity. The mallards are known for their suspicious and chary nature. They're not easily fooled. Yet I have seen mallards throw caution to the wind and literally commit suicide with their foolish behavior. I recall one such incident when I was hunting ducks in a cornfield to which mallards from nearby lakes were coming to feed.

The machine picker had left considerable waste corn and the greenheads were making the most of the opportunity. My partner and I were hunched down among the cornstalks, without blind or other cover, at a spot we knew to be a hot feeding area into which mallards had been dropping the day before. It was almost daylight when we settled in, and in a few minutes we could hear the first mallards coming up from the lake a half mile or so away. Forty or fifty of them were approaching our spot. We froze, expecting them to make their customary circle before pitching in. But no! Those crazy ducks plopped in without so much as a glance or a how-do-you-do at us, so eager were they to get at that yellow corn. This foolhardiness caught us so by surprise that we hardly had time to raise the guns and fire before we were snowed under with flapping wings. Some ducks actually landed almost within arm's reach. It was difficult as well as embarrassing to

shoot ducks at such ridiculous range. They scurried off, but refused to give up. After circling in some confusion, they made another pass at us and attempted to land. Again we were firing at point blank range.

No sooner had these dupes left than another flock came swooping in without the least concern for our very obvious presence. We were sitting in plain sight, in broad daylight. But the ducks kept coming. Flock after flock poured in over us, some were actually stacked up overhead like aircraft at O'Hare Field waiting for their turn to come in. It was a preposterous and wholly unmallardlike situation. The "attacking" attitude of these aggressive mallards almost demoralized us. A couple of times I was so flustered I unknowingly fired both barrels of my double-barreled shotgun simultaneously. It was a nightmare. When the shooting was over, we gathered our limits of beautiful northern greenheads, wondering why these sagacious mallards had abandoned their good sense just to gorge on some corn. Perhaps their greed overwhelmed their better judgment. In that respect they have their counterparts in many people.

Geese have their versions of thrilling air shows too. In spite of their size, the Canada geese are dexterous aerial acrobats. I saw a demonstration of their matchless sense of aerodynamic balance one bitter cold, windy spring day while observing the goose migration in South Dakota.

My companion, Wally Gustafson, and I were shooting pictures of a couple of thousand Canada geese feeding in a stubble field no more than a hundred yards from us. They were moving slowly toward us. As they approached the edge of the field, the high wind lashed at them and, deciding they wanted no more of it, they lifted off. It was a magnificent sight to see them rise into the wind in a solid, flapping, screaming mass. They strained against the howling wind as they moved slowly over us, so close it seemed we could have reached up and grabbed some of those big, black webbed feet. We worked our cameras furiously for a moment, then relaxed to watch. We were only a few hundred feet from a small lake and the geese seemed intent on dropping in there. Rising up on the wind, they wheeled and hovered in a swirling cloud high over the water. A steep bank along shore offered protection from the wind, and this was what they wanted.

Then the thrilling show began. By the hundreds they began tumbling straight down like falling leaves. Side slipping, rolling, volplaning, down, down they fell in a giant shower of outspread wings and glistening bodies. It was like a basket of leaves emptied from the top of a high building. There was no reassuring circle, no maneuvering—they just pulled the rip cords and straight down they all plummeted, breaking their fall with skillful manipulation of wings. In a moment they covered the quiet water in the bay behind the shielding bank. It was a fascinating and remarkable display of the marvelous control and command of aerodynamics that these beautiful birds possess. This one brief spectacle alone was worth all the work and freezing fingers involved in being there on that rugged April morning.

The Ruffed Grouse

Walking slowly down an old logging road one spring morning in the north country, we paused suddenly. What was that sound? We listened with bated breath. There it was again! A far-off hollow rumble, muffled like the distant mutter of thunder. My companion relaxed. "Ruffed grouse drumming," he chuckled, "let's see if we can find him."

We struck off quietly through the brush in the general direction from which the drumming came, pausing now and then to listen for the familiar thumping and get our bearings. We were getting close. Then, as we crept to the edge of a small clearing cluttered with windfalls, we spotted him. Strutting pompously up and down an old spruce log, tail fanned like a peacock, crest bristled, neck feathers ruffed, there was our ruffed grouse, hissing loudly at some imaginary challenger. We watched in silent admiration as this kingly little gentleman of the woodlands gave expression to the urge that the lengthening days of spring demand of male grouse. Now, leaning back on his fantail, he cupped his wings and began to beat the air, slowly at first, then faster and faster until they vanished in a blur. The rapid strokes made a hollow thumping sound that seemed to fill the woods with the muffled drum roll . . bup . . bup . . bup . . bup bup-bup-bup-up-urrrrr. This pulsating flourish is the grouse's way of warning all rivals that he has staked out a territory here and aims to defend it against all comers. It also serves to call the hens interested in mating and fulfilling their desire to brood a clutch of eggs and rear a family of youngsters through the summer.

Grateful to our little drummer for his demonstration, we retreated as quietly as we could. The drumming of the ruffed grouse is one of the commonest sounds in the woods, particularly in the spring, yet many people who frequent the woods have never been conscious of hearing the drumming of the grouse, and fewer still ever actually see the performance.

The ruffed grouse, *Bonasa umbellus,* as a species, ranges over most of North America from the wooded regions of northern Canada and Alaska south to California, Colorado, and east to the Alleghenies and New England. It is a permanent resident, breeding wherever found. There are several related species, and they show geographic color variations, ranging from a red phase along the coasts to gray-browns inland. They are beautifully feathered, and of all the bird kingdom, the ruffed grouse is one of the finer examples of royal bearing, self-reliance, and good looks. It is a bird of the woodlands, with a special preference for the coniferous forests, where it likes to spend the cold winter days snuggled in among the sheltering boughs of spruce trees, eating the nourishing buds.

The grouse hen makes her nest on the ground, beside an old stump, at the base of a tree, or under a windfall. She lays a dozen to fifteen eggs in the hollowed-out duff lined with leaves. As she sits quietly on the nest, her coloration blends perfectly with the spring woodland. When she goes on a brief excursion for food, she skillfully covers the eggs with leaves to escape the attention of a prowling fox, weasel, or other marauder. The young birds, which look like miniature, brown baby chicks, can run as soon as they hatch. Then mama takes full charge of her precocious family until they have learned to forage for their own food and fly well. She is a model parent, and strict disciplinarian, providing devoted care and protection, brooding the little ones under her ruffled feathers at night and on cold rainy days. One of the most pleasant experiences in the summer woods is to see a hen grouse cautiously crossing a woodland road with her tiny family following obediently like little mechanical toys.

Richard Bishop has related to me an interesting roadside encounter he once had with a grouse. "I was driving my jeep along a lumber road," he recalled, "when I saw two balls of fluff dart across the road. I stopped. Almost at once a 'biddie,' as we call a female grouse, marched out of the brush and stopped in the middle of the road. She gave the jeep a dirty look, spread her wings and came at the jeep in a threatening manner, making a complete circle around it. She then clucked and three more balls of fluff crossed the road. She gave the jeep a last dirty look and followed her youngsters into the woods."

As winter approaches in the north country, the grouse grow "snowshoes", comblike projections on the toes, which, spreading under the bird's weight, provide the support they need to travel over the deep snow. When the snow is piled high and temperatures drop to bitter lows, the grouse will fly headlong into a soft drift of snow, burying themselves completely under its protective insulation, and here they spend the night, secure and comfortable. In the morning they burst out of their drift like a bomb and go

SHARP-TAILED GROUSE WITH SHOVELER AND BROOD
By Bob Hines—U.S. Dept. of Interior, Fish and Wildlife Service

about their feeding as usual. The only trouble with this survival plan is that the telltale marks they leave in the snow reveal the grouse's hiding place to the foxes, coyotes, and weasels, who can easily pounce on the bird as it sleeps under the snow. This habit of diving into deep snow can be disastrous if it rains and freezes, making a crust on the snow and lodging, or locking, the bird in the snow.

The ruffed grouse is both a challenge and a delight to the hunter. There is sheer pleasure in quietly walking the old logging roads and forest trails in the early fall mornings, hoping for a clean shot at this elusive little game bird. But it is not all pleasant strolling. Many a pair of boots has been reduced to limp wreckage and its wearer battered to varying degrees of exhaustion in the seasonal quest for the little gentleman of the woodlands. While other game birds are known to challenge the supremacy of the picturesque ruffed grouse, he, nevertheless, holds a distinct, if somewhat indefinable, margin over all competitors.

Hunting grouse is a hair-trigger performance that demands quick reflexes and coordination of steady nerves, for when the startling thunder of grouse wings explodes from underfoot, even a polished hunter can be left standing foolishly in wide-eyed astonishment, too surprised and witless to lift his gun. And should the gunner get gun to shoulder, the grouse is quickly darting and weaving with uncanny skill through the trees, and is out of range in a twinkling. It is not a sport for the lazy hunter, and such a hunter is no match for the grouse. Even the successful grouse hunter dares not weigh the material compensation against the labor incident to the pursuit. But when he stumbles home—weary, tattered and torn—he is happy beyond measure as he displays his bag, small though it may be.

Time to rest (Woodcock)

The American Woodcock

Nature occasionally comes up with some weird creations in the bird world. Yet these oddities are admirably adapted to their environment, perhaps even better than some of their more sophisticated cousins. The pelicans, puffins, and flamingos, for example—all comical lookers, but for a purpose. Then there's the woodcock, *Philohela minor,* Mr. Bigeyes, a strange little introvert veiled in mystery, an oddball for sure, but possessing a charm all his own that appeals to bird watcher and hunter alike.

There's a delightful old Indian legend that describes how the woodcock came to be the quaint bird he is. It is told that when the Creator had grown weary from His long and diligent labors in making the creatures that inhabit the earth, there remained an unsightly little heap of dark brown feathers, a peculiar looking bill, a pair of stumpy legs, and a generous ration of wisdom. Being a thrifty deity, the Creator took up this strange assortment and, with a whimsical smile, made the woodcock. The result was not beautiful. The body was too large for the stumpy legs, and the queer bill was grossly disproportionate. The whole aspect of this creature was that of a sober, big-eyed, shy little creature with an almost inaudible voice and having no song except a musical note made with its wings.

This chunky, almost neckless, short-tailed, warm brown bird with a "dead leaf" pattern, is a bit larger than the bobwhite quail. It has a long, sensitive bill for probing the soil in search of earthworms, its favorite food. A woodcock may consume half its weight in worms in a single day. The upper part of its bill is flexible, enabling the woodcock to open it under the ground, a very ingenious and efficient device. So, you see, nature did have a good reason for giving this chap his odd looking schnozzle. The woodcock's eyes are unusually large for its small head, and are set high and far back, thus enabling it to "look through the back of the head." Thus, while its bill is submerged in the earth, extracting a worm, the woodcock can still keep a sharp lookout on his surroundings for enemies.

Although the woodcock is identified as a shore bird, he is not commonly found along open shores. The woodcock's usual haunt is in the woodlands, swamps, and brushy meadows. He is nocturnal in his activities, spending the day dozing. At night, when the earthworms are most active, he ventures forth. If drought drives the worms far below the surface, he will settle for insect larvae, beetles, seeds, and berries. A series of neat, round holes in the damp ground is a sure sign of a woodcock's presence.

During the courting and nesting season, the male indulges in the curious aerial dance that has long intrigued and mystified ornithologists and other scientists who have sought to discover the source of the woodcock's mating song. The performance usually begins as dusk settles in the woodland opening. The male suddenly spirals up on whistling wings to an altitude of perhaps two hundred feet, where he hovers as the trilling, silvery note — chickaree, chickaree — continues to sound. At the peak of this amazing dance, the woodcock quickly zigzags earthward, sounding short, twittering notes. On the ground he struts like a tom turkey before his admiring mate, then repeats the ecstatic performance again and again. Under a bright moon he may dance all night.

The thrilling whistle of the woodcock's mating "song" is said to be purely instrumental, not his voice, but created by the three outer wing feathers, primaries, which are much narrowed and stiffened. This harplike arrangement, so say the authorities, is what actually produces the unique whistlelike sound as the woodcock soars, hovers, and zigzags through his bewitching nuptial dance. This theory apparently has not been proved conclusively, and some ornithologists are still skeptical. However, it does seem evident that the woodcock has a very limited voice, and is able to utter only a low nasal *beezp* or *peent,* that is suggestive of the call of the nighthawk.

The silvery "song of the woodcock," heard in the eerie silence of a remote, wooded bog· as darkness is falling, has a mystic and disturbing quality that one does not soon forget. I heard it for the first time while camping in northern Minnesota. Near our camp site one quiet evening, a male woodcock gave us a skillful exhibition of his aerial mating dance. Fascinated and awed by this strange little creature of the wild woodlands, we watched and listened for almost an hour, as his frenzied ritual tirelessly went on and on.

The woodcock nests on the ground, well hidden among the leaves and twigs. The three or four hatchlings develop rapidly and are flying in two weeks. Anyone who has observed the woodcock knows how marvelously well camouflaged it is. It can simply vanish among the leaves and brush. One can be looking directly at the very spot where a female woodcock is nesting and not detect the dead leaf pattern of her body.

Woodcocks are considered game birds and are very sporty shooting for the skilled gunner. But they are not hunted as extensively as other game birds, because they are so small and the dense cover in which they are found makes their pursuit difficult and exhausting work. The erratic flight of the woodcock, as it suddenly explodes from underfoot and zigzags off through the trees, not only startles the wits out of the hunter, but also makes it an exciting and elusive target.

I have heard old-time woodsmen claim that woodcocks are reliable forecasters of weather. One old woodcock hunter I once knew told how he had seen migrating woodcock gather in huge flocks along the shore of Lake Superior and sit tight for a day or two. Inevitably, a terrific storm would blow up the day after the woodcock had assembled. The woodcock, sensing the approaching weather front, refused to risk crossing the big lake until the storm passed. I cannot vouch for the truth of this old hunter's story, but he was wise in the ways of the wilderness, and I know the woodcock are imbued with wisdom not common in many birds. Richard Bishop has observed woodcock "pile up" in Cape May County, New Jersey, awaiting a favorable wind to help them fly across Delaware Bay.

The woodcock is found in most of the eastern half of the United States, especially east of the Mississippi, and in the southern portion of Canada from Manitoba eastward to the Atlantic. The woodcock that inhabit the northern regions migrate for the winter down into the Ohio Valley, eastward to New Jersey, and southwestward to Texas.

The Prairie Chicken

Fifty years ago the cackle and booming of the prairie chicken, *Tympanuchus cupido pinnatus,* were still familiar sounds to early-rising farmers across the central plains. One had only to tramp across a stubble or hay field to flush a flock of these plump grouse that bear a close resemblance to the barred rock chickens in the farmers' hen houses. But the pressure of the gun and plow has pushed these colorful symbols of the Old West almost into oblivion. Now, the prairie chicken is almost a rarity in many of the dozen or so prairie states where it once thrived, and only in the Dakotas, Kansas, and Oklahoma are they numerous enough to justify a short hunting season.

The species of the central plains is the greater prairie chicken, also identified as pinnated grouse. A subspecies, the lesser prairie chicken, *Tympanuchus pallidicinctus,* is a smaller, lighter colored bird of limited distribution in the southwest, from western Kansas down to northern Texas.

The early colonists found the heath hen, an eastern species of the prairie chicken, now extinct, plentiful and owed many a meal to these good eating fowl. The ornithologists tell us there were no prairie chickens on the central plains when the first explorers came through. The bird, they say, originated east of the Alleghenies, but began extending its range westward about the time early settlers were coming into the prairie country. By 1850, the chickens were abundant throughout the central plains. They loved the open range, the big open spaces, and the lush grasslands. Their numbers increased tremendously until they began to disappear from many areas where relentless hunting and mechanized farming were more than they could cope with. Only with the help of strict hunting laws and better land use has the prairie chicken been able to hang on to its meager remnants. More farmers now exercise caution in mowing hay fields and plowing land where prairie chickens nest, and do less spring and fall burning of the meadows and grasslands, so important to the welfare of prairie chickens.

The prairie chicken hen seeks out her nesting site in the dense grass of the meadows and in the thickets along fence lines. She forms a well-hidden hollow in which she lays a dozen or so brown-flecked olive eggs. The chicks hatch in three weeks, are

able to run almost immediately, and can fly in two weeks. They scurry around the fields, foraging for all sorts of bugs, seeds, berries, and grains. They develop rapidly and are completely feathered in six weeks if they manage to survive the many dangers that constantly threaten their lives. Many young chicks are caught by snakes, hawks, owls, crows, magpies, badgers, skunks, coyotes, and foxes. Many are killed on the roads by speeding cars, by farm machinery harvesting grain, and hay mowers. By September less than half of the chicks are left. Thus we can see that, faced with so many natural and man-made hazards, the plight of the prairie chicken is discouraging, to say the least.

As an Iowa farm boy, I had many opportunities to observe the prairie chickens that were quite plentiful at that time in our area. A large flock was usually somewhere in our fields the year round. And many mornings in the spring we could hear the cocks cackling and booming in the pasture just north of our buildings. This seemed to be their favorite booming ground, and it was fun to watch them from the cover of our grove only a few yards away. I recall my amazement the first time I saw the booming cocks inflate those bright orange air sacs that popped out like toy balloons from the sides of the neck. While I had heard their booming many times, until then I had not been aware that the sound was accomplished with these weird drums.

The mating dance of the prairie chicken has been described many times, and perhaps with some exaggeration. On the farm, I watched this interesting ritual several times and while it is a lively affair, I do not remember seeing the bloody cock-fighting that some observers report.

For a week or more in April, several males would come to our pasture early in the morning. Each seemed to have his private territory staked out, which he fiercely defended against all male intruders. Here he would strut and display himself and prance about like a foot stamping Indian dancer. At intervals he would erect his spread tail straight up, thrust his head forward, ruffle his wing feathers, and stamp his feet on the ground so rapidly that he could be heard some distance away. As this took place, the vivid orange air sacs on his neck began to swell like a Scottish bagpipe and the feather tufts on his head would pop up like satanic horns. His whole attitude was one of savage belligerence. Then came that deep-pitched hollow who-hoo-hoo booming from the tightly inflated air sacs. If there were any hens around, the excited males would make crouching runs at each other like jousting knights, flapping their wings, leaping and throwing spurs in the manner of game cocks. But the fighting seemed only a token effort to impress the hens. I cannot recall seeing any of the cocks really fighting it out in a deadly duel. When a hen finally selected her favorite male and mated, she went off about the more serious business of finding a suitable nesting site, and until the next spring she had no further interest in the ceremonious males.

Winters were always tough on the prairie chicken. But they stayed on. In those days when there were prairie chickens in Minnesota, many of these northerners would move down into Iowa and Missouri for the winter.

Many midwinter mornings on the farm the prairie chickens would fly in and roost in the trees in our grove, seeking shelter from the wind, deep snow, and bitter cold. They looked like ordinary chickens, cackling and clucking among themselves. When the snow was deep and little feed available for the birds, my dad would scatter bundles of oats from our grain stacks and lay out piles of cracked corn on boards, a friendly gesture the prairie chickens seemed to appreciate. They would come right in and spend the day happily gobbling up every morsel. Through the winter they became quite accustomed to our presence. But as soon as the weather warmed, they were off and away, wild as ever.

I hunted prairie chicken a few times, but always had mixed emotions about shooting these attractive residents that seemed part of our farm scene. They were easy to shoot if you could get within range. But they were cagey, and always had sentries staked out. They fly swiftly with a rapid, fluttering wing beat, pausing at short intervals to sail, then flutter, sail, flutter. I found the best time to hunt them was on a very windy day. Prairie chickens detest wind and they would seek shelter from it on the lee side of a knoll, and sit there throughout the day. It was then quite easy to stalk them, as they seemed reluctant to fly up and struggle against the wind. I shot my first prairie chicken on such a day. Spotting a large flock sitting on the lee side of a low hill in our stubble field, I crept within easy range and selected what seemed like a big male. I'm sure they saw me, but they sat tight until I stood up. I fired and down came my rooster. The next day at the dinner table he looked very appetizing on the platter, but we soon discovered that I had probably killed the oldest and toughest rooster in the flock.

It is a sad thing to see such big, hearty fowl of the prairie slowly fade from the scene. We cannot restore their long gone grasslands and meadows, but hopefully, we can keep intact those limited numbers now scattered here and there.

204

Ring-Necked Pheasant

In our world of wildfowl the continuing decline of many species is a tragic trend that we would hope some day, somehow, may be stemmed. We do, however, have a pleasant reversal of these circumstances in the ring-necked pheasant, *Phasianus colchicus torquatus,* a gaudy import from China that took to the American scene as easily as ducks to water. After many unsuccessful attempts to introduce European pheasants in the eastern United States, a very successful introduction of the Chinese ringneck was made in Oregon in 1881. The bird quickly adapted to its new environment and increased so rapidly that ten years later the state declared a seventy-five-day hunting season and hunters took fifty thousand pheasants opening day.

Since then the ringneck has been introduced in most states, and is found in at least forty-one of these states, including Alaska and Hawaii. In spite of all the curves that a mechanized society can throw at this oriental beauty, he thrives. Heavy hunting, unfavorable climate, destruction of habitat, and a host of natural enemies cannot keep him down. With a liking for the farm country of the grain belt and the prairies, the pheasant has become a popular, if not the leading, game bird in many north central states. In South Dakota alone a million and a half birds are taken each fall by hunters. In 1946 that state's total take by hunters was seven and a half million pheasants!

The original home of all pheasants is Asia, from the Black Sea on the west to Japan on the east. There are more than a hundred species and subspecies, and among them are some of the most gorgeously adorned birds in the world. Our domesticated chickens are descended from pheasant ancestors, as are the peacock and guinea hen. The roots of the pheasants go very deep, and archaeologists have traced the ring-necked pheasant back 25 million years into the era of the giant mammoth and saber-toothed tiger.

The pheasant cock in his full springtime plumage is a worthy example of oriental splendor. Certainly he is one of the world's most exotic fowls. Yellow bill, iridescent green head with black ear tufts like little horns, brilliant red cheek patches, neckband of pure white, and a body superbly and intricately patterned in metallic bronze, brown, gold, copper, gray, and black, including a long tail gracefully pointed. The hen is far less spectacular and rather subdued, as most female birds are. Nevertheless, she is an attractive bird. If you are in pheasant country in the spring you can hear the cocks crowing in the early morning as they begin their daily warm-up to capture a share of the hens for their harem. Their crowing has a slight resemblance to that of the barnyard rooster. They flap their wings and emit a loud kok-kok that is at least an attempt to imitate the domestic rooster's cock-a-doodle-do.

While the cock birds are at their spendid best in the spring, they engage in a courtship that is as weird and aggressive as that of the grouse. The cock struts proudly before the hens, displaying himself at every angle like a fashion model. He puffs up, walks with a ridiculously exaggerated bobbing motion, then dances in little circles, drags a wing and generally puts on a most seductive show, hopeful of luring a sizable number of hens into his harem. The harem may contain five or more hens. He is a ferocious fighter in mating season, and when challenged by other cocks, can wield his sharp spurs with bloody effectiveness, if necessary, to drive off roosters attempting to steal his hens.

The mated hen immediately sneaks away into the hay fields, slough grass, or weed patches along fence lines to make her nest. She will incubate six to a dozen or more eggs. Some cooperative-minded hens double up on one nest and share the responsibilities of incubating. An alarming number of hens and nests in hay fields are destroyed by mowers. Many farmers now attach a flushing bar to scare off the hens ahead of the sickle bar. This saves the hen, but usually the nest and eggs are destroyed. If this occurs during the hen's egg-laying period, she will usually renest. Only one brood is raised during a summer.

The pheasant chicks are ready to scramble out of the nest soon after hatching. They are then well able to run about and follow the hen as they hunt for insects, seeds, grains, berries, or whatever is available. The pheasant diet is omnivorous; they'll eat almost anything. The young ones can fly in two weeks. The hen stays with them until they are at least twelve weeks old. The roosters may stay in the vicinity of their harems but they make no contribution to raising the brood.

There have been complaints that heavy pheasant populations drive out or usurp the place of the native upland game birds, such as quail and prairie chickens. And farmers sometimes have serious problems with massive flocks of pheasants destroying young corn and other crops.

While the pheasant has generally prospered in a fantastic way over a wide area of the prairie states, it has some bad years. When winters are especially severe or torrential spring rains flood out nests, the annual crop drops quickly and sometimes disastrously. Many states do some stocking of pheasants to compensate for these winter losses. Many pheasants starve and freeze to death in the northern prairie regions when heavy snowfall combines with prolonged sub-zero temperatures. Sportsmen's clubs and other conservation groups usually come to the rescue at such times and run chains of feeding stations for storm-bound pheasants. The mortality rate of pheasants seems discouragingly high. Predators and disease kill off enormous numbers. A hen is lucky if she has half of her brood by fall. But in spite of the heavy toll, the ring-neck is tenacious and hardy enough to maintain a heavy population in those areas where ample cover and food are available.

Today's cock pheasant is a smart bird and worthy game. He has learned to survive by wits and evasive tactics when hordes of hunters are beating the bush for him. He knows how to skulk and hide, permitting hunters to pass within inches. He can run almost as fast as a horse and delights in cutting around a line of hunters or sneaking back through the lines. When he flushes, he explodes with such a clatter of wings and screaming cackles that he can unnerve the most experienced gunner. If wounded, he can vanish instantly in grass or stubble no more than four inches high and scoot away undetected. He can drive talented retrieving dogs crazy with his hide-and-seek strategy. In the years that this naturalized citizen has been with us, he has learned all the tricks of survival, and he employs them with admirable skill. More power to him, and long may he live!

Bobwhite, Cheerful Little Whistler

One of the many pleasant memories of my boyhood on the farm is the delightful piping of the bobwhite, *Colinus virginiana,* calling lustily from his perch atop a fence post, as we rode the corn cultivators up and down the sun-drenched fields. His clear, ringing "bob-white" whistle brightened the dull monotony of our wearisome work. All through the morning he would cheerfully serenade us, as though sensing that his efforts were appreciated.

Bobwhites were not plentiful in our area at that time. We seldom had more than a covey or two around the farm, but we cherished these few and did all we could to encourage them to remain. In the winter, those that had survived the summer and fall would occasionally come fluttering into the farmyard to enjoy the luxury of cracked grain, which we kept laid out for them. On the coldest days we could expect them early in the morning for breakfast, and they would stay nearby through the day. They were never really tame, but they manifested a gentle, friendly, and trusting nature. We loved them dearly, and to hunt and shoot them was, for me, unthinkable. I would as soon have shot down the songbirds. It has been several years since I last heard a bobwhite whistle, but I still associate the memory with the rich aroma of the growing cornfields, new-mown hay, and the sweet fragrance of early summer meadows.

In addition to the bobwhite, there are five other quail species native to the United States. These include Gambel's quail, a western species; California quail; scaled quail of the southwest; mountain quail of the Sierras and Rockies; and the harlequin of Arizona and Texas. All of these species have limited regional distribution in the west and southwest, whereas the bobwhite is found in thirty-eight states, thirty-six of which permit quail hunting. The heaviest concentration of bobwhites is now in about fourteen states — Nebraska, Kansas, Oklahoma, Arkansas, Missouri, Illinois, Kentucky, Tennessee, the Carolinas, New Jersey, Delaware, Florida and Georgia.

The bobwhite is the friendliest and most engaging of all the prairie fowl. He loves the meadows, farmlands, orchards, and

Through the timber (Mallards)
Reproduced by permission of Richard E. Bishop

209

grainfields, especially where sufficient brush, weedy fences, and hedgerows are available to provide the cover and protection quail require. At one time the bobwhite was plentiful everywhere throughout the United States east of the Rockies, but as farms were cleared of brush, and since the era of big-scale mechanized farms, the bobwhite has either decreased in many areas or disappeared entirely.

The colonists and early settlers were grateful for the numerous quail that provided them a staple food item. And through the years, the bobwhite has been a major attraction for hunters. In the south, where quail hunting has been a tradition as firmly entrenched as the Democratic party, the sport has reached an aristocratic refinement beyond compare. Every section of quail country has its methods of hunting bobwhite, but one essential everywhere is the use of well-trained bird dogs, fast rangers with bird sense, good noses, and the capacity to tirelessly cover many acres of quail ground. In the south, many hunters are mounted on sturdy horses and follow the dogs and their trainer from covey to covey.

The thrilling aspect of the quail hunt is that nerve-tingling moment when a covey bursts from a thicket ahead of the pointing bird dog. With an electrifying whir of wings, they explode in all directions, like fragments of a bursting bomb. The whirring of their wings, when flushed, is evidently a defensive action in an effort to frighten the enemy, because quail *can* fly quite silently.

In fall and winter, the bobwhites range in coveys which are usually family groups — the mated pair and their summer brood. The family stays together through the winter, roosting at night in thick cover. Quail have a curious habit of roosting on the ground in a tight, circular formation with bodies packed closely together, heads facing out, and tails toward the center. This seems to afford both warmth and a defense against predators. When startled, they erupt in all directions, each flying straight away without colliding. It is an effective action that confuses the enemy, when they vanish to all points of the compass. A covey that has been flushed will usually fly only short distances. The scattered birds are soon calling to each other with their special rallying signals, and in a few minutes are gathered again.

The winter in the more northerly states are difficult times for bobwhite, who is reluctant to leave for warmer country. Drifting snow will bury whole coveys, as they huddle in their compact little circles. This is good protection for them unless freezing sleet forms a tough crust and traps them. One spring I found the remains of such a tragedy on our farm. The melting snow revealed the decimated bodies of a covey, lying almost as they had been roosting when the storm sealed their doom.

Under the best conditions, less than 50 percent of the fall quail population survives the first winter. Of all the winter birds that braved the cold winter on our farm, the bobwhite seemed the most vulnerable and least able to successfully forage in the deep snow for seeds and other food, much of which was under snow and ice for many weeks. These were harsh times, not only for the bobwhite, but also for the pheasants and prairie chickens. On days when winter was at its worst, all of these fowl sought refuge among our trees and looked for the handouts of cracked grain they came to expect at such times of crises.

In the spring, the bobwhite engages in a nuptial courtship similar to that of the ruffed grouse. The usually mild mannered cocks suddenly become pugnacious little demons, who fight and quarrel fiercely among themselves as they compete for the favor of the females. Bobwhites are monogamous. The attachment between mates is very strong, and a pair usually remains together for more than a year. But the young cocks must find mates, and they make a great show of displaying themselves. During this time, they not only engage in considerable fighting, but also whistle their hearts out. Once mated, the male remains relatively quiet during the nesting season and does not whistle. The cheery whistlers heard during the summer are usually males that failed to win a mate, so they have nothing to do but whistle.

The mated pairs go off by themselves and seek out a suitable nesting site. The nest is built in grassy growth in open areas or along the edges of thickets. The male, unlike most fowl, is an attentive helper at this time and throughout the nesting period. He hollows out a depression for the nest and lines it with leaves and grass, arranging an arched roof for better concealment. After all the eggs are laid—anywhere from a dozen to twenty-two—either the hen or the cock incubates them while the other mate remains nearby. Usually the hen tends the nest.

When the chicks are hatched, the cock immediately joins the family group and takes full part in the various duties. He will even take over complete care of the brood if the hen should disappear or die. Only one brood is reared in a summer. The young leave the nest at once, and the entire family goes forth to range through the fields and meadows, staying close together day and night. They eat all sorts of weed seeds, grains, berries, fruit, vegetables, worms, and insects. Were it not for the exceptionally large broods the bobwhite rears, the species would never have survived as well as it has.

The variegated plumage of the bobwhite gives him excellent protective camouflage, and he is an expert at employing it when, in the face of danger, he instantly freezes in the grass or foliage of the thickets, where he is practically invisible.

It is unfortunate that so few of us in this generation have had the heart-warming pleasure of hearing the cheery call of the bobwhite, as its clearly enunciated notes ring out in the still air of a lovely summer morning on the prairie. Such simple joys as this can be miraculous therapy for troubled spirits in these times of eroding values and environment. Hopefully, the bobwhite's dwindling numbers are not on their way to join the vanished ranks of the heath hen and passenger pigeon.

SCOUTING FOR FOOD (FULVOUS TREE DUCKS)
By Bob Hines—U.S. Dept. of Interior, Fish and Wildlife Service

The Wild Turkey

The American wild turkey, *Meleagris gallapavo silvestris,* has been so much a part of our country's history and tradition that it could well have been our national bird. Ben Franklin campaigned vigorously to have the turkey proclaimed our national symbol, but lost the battle to the bald eagle. The turkey is fine eating and an interesting fowl, but has neither the appearance nor the personality to be a worthy symbol for America.

The Pilgrims and early colonists found the wild turkey plentiful, but this abundance was not destined to continue. Connecticut hunters shot the last turkey in that state in 1813, and Massachusetts hunters saw their last turkey in 1851.

The turkey is our largest game bird and is distinctively American. The big bronzed gobblers were strutting throughout the New World long before the white man arrived. The Aztecs had domesticated the turkey in that region long before the Spaniards came to Mexico, where the turkey was also abundant. Turkeys were taken back and introduced to Europe by Cortez in 1530, and within a decade Europeans were enjoying turkey dinners. So the Pilgrims, coming here in 1620, probably were already familiar with this delectable fowl, and we can imagine their joy at finding it so plentiful in America.

Although the wild turkey has disappeared from eighteen of the thirty-six states where it once ranged, the domesticated versions of wild turkeys have become America's greatest contributor to animal husbandry. The yearly hatch of over 100 million turkey poults is big business.

There is some confusion over how the turkey got its name. One theory is that in Europe it was confused with the guinea hen, an African fowl that had been brought to Europe by way of the Turkish Empire. Both the new bird from the New World and the guinea hen from Turkey were called "turkey." Another theory is that the name derives from the bird's call, which sounds like "turk-turk-turk."

When the explorers and early settlers moved westward, the turkey seemed to be everywhere in the woodland areas. It was a substantial part of their diet. In those days, and for some years

213

following the settlement of the west, the turkey ranged from western Nebraska, Oklahoma, and Texas eastward to the Atlantic, and from southern Ontario south to the Gulf and Florida. But overshooting, clearing of the open woodlands, and loss of many of the nut trees—especially the chestnut—gradually eliminated it from much of its original northwestern range and in other places where the pressure of increasing population drove the turkey out.

In some sections of the deep south, turkey hunting has continued to be a popular sport on the larger farms and plantations where owners have given the birds protection and carefully supervise the hunting. But the turkey flocks are generally quite limited, compared to the early days. For years, not more than twenty-one states have had any turkeys. However, restocking and intensive management have brought them back to the point where twenty-nine states now have limited open season on turkeys. Some states recently have had an open season on turkeys for the first time in sixty years. Game management groups have great difficulty making turkeys, hatched in an incubator, wild enough to have a natural fear of man.

One interesting restocking program is being carried on by the Florida Game Fish and Fresh Water Commission. That state has more than tripled its wild turkey population by restocking. Thousands of birds for restocking are raised each year, under careful management, in natural habitat. As the birds mature, they are trapped and distributed around the state. Some are released from small planes, flying at very low altitude and reduced speed over areas inaccessible to ground transportation. Florida's program is also supplying restocking turkeys to other states, including Texas, Louisiana, North Carolina, and Maryland.

The wild turkey population in the United States, now that it is being more carefully managed as a game crop, is estimated to be about a half million.

The turkey is not migratory, but early accounts tell of large flocks migrating long distances on foot, looking for the fallen acorns and other nuts they depended on for their staple food. Acorns are the turkey's first love, and they will gorge themselves when the crop is sufficient. When there are no nuts, they eat all sorts of bugs, berries, wild fruit, grass, and seeds, foraging through the countryside and woods like a herd of cows. Some turkeys like the mountain slopes, some the swamps, and others the open woodlands. But their common need is a tall tree in which to roost. It is quite a sight in the southern states to see a flock of big gobblers bedded down high up in the top of a big pine tree. Their great size makes them appear rather incongruous perched so high, but they seem to feel more secure there than in the lower branches.

The toms and hens separate in the fall and do not associate during the winter. They may roost in nearby trees, but the toms flock together and the hens stay to themselves with their young poults from the summer hatch. But with the arrival of spring, the propagating impulse turns the turkey woods into a bedlam of noise. Morning after morning the courtship ritual of the toms is a hullabaloo of discordant gobbling, as they express their individual interests in establishing a harem of two or three choice hens. At the slightest provocation the affair can quickly degenerate into a bloody brawl, in which a luckless tom can be left trampled and stone dead after taking a barrage of skull-cracking pecks from a vicious adversary, who may have been his companionable roosting partner all through the winter months. The rivalry goes on every morning during the mating season. The toms begin their lusty gobbling and strutting, with tails fanned, wings dragging, breasts puffed up like fat pillows, as the hens gather to watch, trying to decide which gobbler they should choose to father their summer brood. When the first hen appears on the scene, a gobbler will sound off, and the others will instantly come charging in, all gobbling excitedly, their wattles gorged with blood, and heads livid red, blue and white. They all join in the big strutting act, competing for the hens' attention. But the silly toms, so engrossed with their displaying and jealous watching of their challengers, pay more attention to each other than to the hens. When a hen finally is ready to accept her favorite tom, she literally must throw herself at his feet before he will allow himself to be diverted from his self-centered pomposity.

The tom usually strives to win two or three hens for his harem, and for this privilege he may have to subdue quite a number of his fellow toms and sustain a rash of bloody wounds.

After mating, the hen quietly slips away to nest. She wants to find a well concealed place that offers maximum protection. She wants to not only avoid predators, but also the tom. Her mate, the arrogant lout, if he discovers the nest, will crush every egg for the selfish purpose of prolonging his sexual enjoyments. So the hen cleverly devises a nest beside a log, in a thicket or briar patch, but always in a dry place, because her poults cannot endure a wet nesting place.

The hen will lay from eight to fifteen eggs. When leaving or approaching the nest, she uses extreme caution not to reveal herself and seldom uses the same course twice, because she knows that a devilish crow could be silently watching nearby and would immediately remove and eat the eggs.

Audubon, in his writings, says that several turkey hens may join forces—possibly for their mutual safety—and lay their eggs in one nest. He once observed three hens sitting on forty-two eggs! When the eggs, after incubating twenty-eight days, are ready to hatch, the hen will not leave the nest under any circumstance. The hen and her poults, as they forage for food during the summer, are in constant danger from a host of predators who relish turkey meat—foxes, skunks, bobcats, crows, owls, hawks, dogs, cats, and of course skulking human poachers.

For several weeks after hatching, the poults huddle at night under the feathers of the hen. They are extremely sensitive to cold, and a chilling rain can wipe out an entire brood. A turkey that is strong enough and smart enough to evade the guns and predators can live as long as twelve years. Some toms grow to weigh thirty-five pounds.

The tom and his two or three hens remain in the same vicinity through the nesting season. As soon as the brood comes off the nest, the hens flock together and remain aloof from the toms, who would, in their persistence, harass and even kill the young poults if given the opportunity. Eventually, the toms go off together and do not molest the hens until the next spring.

In the South, turkey hunting is conducted in the neighborly and genteel manner typical of the sportsmen of that region. There are various ways to hunt turkey. One common way is to drive them through the swamps or woods into the path of waiting hunters. Other hunters, wise to the ways of the old gobbler, prefer to use a turkey call and talk a big fellow within gun range. This method requires infinite patience and considerable skill.

On the wing, a gobbler has unbelievably sharp eyesight and can perceive the slightest motion at a great distance. And he can outrun a horse, as Audubon learned when, on horseback, he chased a tom turkey several hours without success.

The current status of the wild turkey is looking up, as the turkey states continue to show increasing interest in sustained stocking programs and intensive management of their expanding flocks. Although much of the turkey's natural range has been destroyed, there is still enough suitable turkey country remaining to support many birds. With some luck we may again hear old tom sounding off in those woodlands where his yelping call has not been heard for many decades.

(continued on page 225)

START OF DAY

Mallards *(Anas p. platyhrynchos)*

217

RIGHT ON TIME

218

Common Canada Geese *(Branta canadensis canadensis)*

A LONER

Roseate Spoonbill (*Ajaia ajaja*)

219

THE SEARCH FOR FOOD

White Ibis *(Eudocimus albus)*

FLYING HIGH

Woodcock *(Philohela minor)*

221

GRACEFUL FLIGHT

Whistling Swans *(Olar columbianus)*

WHITE MAJESTY

American Egret *(Casmerodius albus egretta)*

223

A PROMISING BAY

Mallards (*Anas p. platyhrynchos*)

HARLEQUIN DUCK
By Bob Hines—U.S. Dept. of Interior,
Fish and Wildlife Service

THE GREAT WILDLIFE REFUGES

A pair of disgruntled duck hunters quietly watched a great flock of mallards drift high over their blind, well out of gun range, then suddenly cascade into the marsh a mile away, where the familiar flying-goose signs marked the boundary of a national wildlife refuge. The happy jabbering of thousands of ducks and geese drifted tantalizingly across the water as the luckless hunters listened and watched more high flying ducks go over and pitch eagerly into the refuge. The ducks knew that behind those signs there was safety from the booming guns, as well as ample food and a place to rest undisturbed as long as they desired to stay.

The unhappy hunters, finally calling it a day, picked up the decoys and left. They somehow resented the refuge and its magnetic power to pull the ducks and geese down from their high-flying, leaving the once attractive points and passes on nearby lakes far less productive after the first day or two of open season shooting. There were other hunters there that day who also had poor shooting, but who were quietly pleased. They were glad to see the waterfowl coming in such great numbers. They could recall the time—before the refuge was established—when the ducks and geese would have long since been burned out of the area by the army of hunters that converged on every likely and unlikely piece of ground to pour shot at all waterfowl in sight, from dawn to dusk. Now, the birds were not only here in abundance, but were lingering until cold weather drove them southward. And on some days when the weather was right, the constant coming and going of the waterfowl on the refuge provided the patient hunters with some good shooting.

Our wildlife refuges, both national and state-managed, have increased over the years to where they now are major contributors to the preservation of both habitat and wildlife. In the United States we now have 220 national waterfowl refuges, covering over 2.5 million acres of marsh and water. In addition there are over 66,000 acres of potholes and marshes, production areas for waterfowl, acquired in scattered locations in fifty-seven counties of the Dakotas, Minnesota and Nebraska. Fifty-eight of these national refuges are open to waterfowl hunting.

The various states are also providing waterfowl management and conservation areas that are of great importance to the refuge system. Now in operation are 1,360 such refuge areas, covering about 4.5 million acres.

Our waterfowl problems really did not begin until about 1900. Until that time the ducks and geese prospered. The country was one big refuge for birds and other animals, and they were kept in balance by nature with water, open land, and plenty of food everywhere. But as the nation grew, the axe, plough, and shotgun began to take a devastating toll. Then came the automatic shotgun, better ammunition, and an increase in market hunting. The situation became desperate, and many people were genuinely alarmed at what was happening to the waterfowl and all species of wildlife. The first and most historic step taken in defense of wildfowl was the signing, in 1916, of the International Migratory Bird Treaty, involving Canada and the United States, to protect

Time to eat (Canada's Pitching Geese)

Reproduced by permission of Richard E. Bishop

and regulate the taking of migratory birds. The treaty was ratified by Congress in 1918. Still, the number of waterfowl continued to dwindle. Drought, hunting pressure, and drainage of wetlands took a mounting toll of all species of wildfowl.

Our national wildlife refuge program had its beginning when President Theodore Roosevelt established the Pelican Island refuge in Florida, in 1903, for the protection of the brown pelican and other birds that nest in colonies. Interest in refuges grew, and by 1908 a total of thirty-nine national wildlife refuges had been set aside, primarily for protection of colonial nesting species.

The waterfowl refuge idea got a big boost in 1924, when Congress appropriated funds for the purchase of bottomlands along the upper Mississippi River. This created the Upper Mississippi River Wildlife and Fish Refuge, extending from Wabasha, Minnesota, to Rock Island, Illinois. This preserved a strategic area of the Mississippi flyway habitat that was being swallowed up by the many developments of our growing nation. Today, this is a valuable habitat for countless waterfowl and provides good fishing, hunting, and recreation for millions of people who live within easy driving distance of this region. This was the first refuge in which public hunting was authorized.

Another important refuge was authorized by Congress in 1928, when the Bear River Migratory Bird Refuge was established on the delta where the Bear River flows out of Great Salt Lake. It produces thousands of waterfowl each year. Parts of this refuge are open to public hunting.

Progress in waterfowl and habitat conservation continued as Congress, in 1929, created the Migratory Conservation Act, which was based on the International Treaty. It provided for enlarged federal conservation operations, strengthened enforcement of federal regulations, hunting seasons, and bag limits and authorized a system of waterfowl refuges.

But 1929 was the beginning of the disastrous drought years. As choking dust storms howled across the central plains, potholes, marshes, and wetlands dried up. Waterfowl shriveled to a dismally low point. As the drought years went on unabated, and waterfowl all but vanished by 1934, the situation clearly demonstrated the need for better conservation of water resources and breeding grounds. Through the influence of a special duck commission appointed by President Franklin Roosevelt, an ambitious program of rehabilitating habitat and purchasing land was launched. This proved so successful that the idea was continued and expanded to purchase and restore more habitat for wildlife. The Migratory

Bird Hunting Stamp Act, better known as "duck stamp," was enacted in 1934. Every duck hunter was required to purchase the one-dollar stamp and have it in possession while hunting. This provided additional funds for developing the refuge program. The duck stamp was increased to two dollars in 1949, and to three dollars in 1958. Duck stamps must, by law, be signed and thus canceled by the owner.

Chains of new refuges now began to spot the flyways from coast to coast, each providing sanctuary where migratory birds could rest and feed and, in the north, find suitable nesting places. In the south, the refuges were safe wintering quarters that supplied every need for both ducks and geese.

The waterfowl in all four major flyways have made good use of the refuges. Many species are beginning to use some refuges exclusively, either for wintering or for nesting, in preference to other areas where food is less plentiful or where hunting pressure drives them out.

Along the Atlantic flyway, migratory waterfowl stop to rest and feed at the coastal refuges from Maine to Florida. The greater snow goose population of the Atlantic flyway now winters mainly on four national refuges — Back Bay, Chincoteague, Mackay Island, and Pea Island. Large flocks also rest at Fortescue, New Jersey, which is not a national refuge. Many of the brant in the Atlantic flyway are now wintering at the Brigantine refuge in New Jersey.

The Canada geese of the Mississippi flyway are now stopping short in their southbound flight and are wintering in the more northerly refuges, such as the Horicon marsh in Wisconsin, Crab Orchard in Illinois, Reelfoot and Tennessee refuges, and the state-owned management areas in southern Illinois and Kentucky.

The Canada goose flock from the eastern prairies of Canada is now concentrating on the more northerly Swan Lake and Squaw Creek refuges in Missouri.

The Canada geese of the Central flyway are now using the Lower Souris, Sand Lake, Tewaukon, and Salt Plains refuges in the Dakotas.

Ninety percent of all waterfowl in the Pacific flyway are now concentrated on refuges such as the Bear River, Tule-Klamath Lake, Sacramento, Caluso, Sutter, Merced, and Delaware.

The popularity of the northern refuges has created a strange problem that game management people did not anticipate. More geese are changing their centuries-old habits and are abandoning their ancestral wintering haunts in the deep south. As the more

CANVASBACKS AND WHISTLING SWANS
By Bob Hines—U.S. Dept. of Interior, Fish and Wildlife Service

northerly refuges have developed, the geese are showing a decided preference for these, as long as the food is ample and sufficient water remains open through the winter months. As the geese continue in increasing numbers to forsake their traditional wintering grounds in the gulf and coastal regions, they build up heavy concentrations in the northern refuges. This is disturbing to wildlife authorities who prefer a wider distribution of the populations, and better use of all the southern refuge areas. Biologists have resorted to all sorts of devices and strategy to discourage so many geese from coming into the northern refuges and to lure some of them back to their warmer wintering grounds. But the geese will have none of it. They are determined not to fly any farther south than necessary, as long as they can secure food and protection in the north. Geese have been captured at the Illinois state refuge on Horseshoe Lake in Illinois and trucked south in cages to the Mississippi Delta refuge. It was reported that the geese beat the truck back home.

The problem is compounded by the biological fact that it takes only a few years for a goose to forget its ancestral wintering ground. The custom is passed from generation to generation by the older birds who lead the flocks south. As the young birds learn the way, they lead succeeding generations. Thus, as the migration flights end at the northerly refuges, the younger geese never learn of the southern marshes. As the older geese, who once knew the southern wintering regions, die, there are no geese left to take the flocks into those forgotten places far to the south. The day may be near when the call of the wild geese will no longer be heard in the southern states.

Some of the refuges have saved birds from total extinction. The rare whooping crane, once down to only fourteen birds, was given winter sanctuary in the Aransas refuge in Texas. Though the whooping crane has not prospered, the population has slowly increased to at least three dozen.

The trumpeter swan was down to only seventy-three birds in 1939 in the Centennial Valley and Yellowstone National Park. The Red Rock Lakes National Wildlife Refuge, established in 1935 in Montana, has helped the trumpeter achieve a comeback.

The refuge system not only provides comfortable and secure living for all species of migratory waterfowl, but also furnishes hunting for many sportsmen in the six hundred thousand acres that are made available to hunters in fifty-eight refuges. The refuge system is based on the idea that refuges are for the use and enjoyment of the American public — for all of us. Many refuges are offering this enjoyment of the wildlife through visitor centers, nature trails, picnic, hunting, and fishing areas. The success of the refuge system in preserving water, land, and habitat for wildlife emphasizes the need to continue expanding the program as rapidly as possible to offset the drainage of wetlands, damming of streams, and all the other detrimental factors that are constantly eating away at the places where our wildlife can safely hide, live, and rear their young.

BLUE-WINGED TEAL
By Bob Hines—U.S. Dept. of Interior,
Fish and Wildlife Service

ATTRACTING WATERFOWL
AND GAME BIRDS

Imagine the joy and satisfaction of a group of 4-H Club youngsters as they observe a pair of Canada geese busily taking possession of a nesting site the club had constructed on a small farm
pond as a nature project. With the help of the agriculture extension agent and the local game warden, the club had constructed
three washtub nesting sites on a farmer's pond where migrating
Canadas occasionally stopped briefly to rest and feed. The club
was hopeful that the man-made habitat would entice a pair or two
of geese to remain and occupy the nests.

It was an exciting day for the club when the game warden
called the club leader to report that a mated pair of Canadas on
the pond was apparently settling in one of the washtub nests. The
venture had paid off. Later in the season, when the goslings were
off the nest, there were many interesting excursions to the pond
to watch the two beautiful adult birds and their growing family.

The success and rewarding experience this 4-H Club achieved
is just a small example of how youth groups, as well as adult organizations and individuals, can make useful and important contributions to improving and creating suitable habitat for many
species of waterfowl and game birds.

Wildfowl can be attracted to almost any area by offering them
an inviting habitat that provides ample water, food, suitable cover, nesting material, and protection from predators and intruders.

For years sportsmen's clubs have been planting vegetation as
food and cover for waterfowl and upland game birds. This is the
surest way to bring back the ducks, geese, and other birds to
those places where adequate feed and cover have disappeared, or
perhaps never existed.

If you live in an area where there is a slough, pond, lake, or
stream and would like to see some ducks or geese dropping in
during their migration, or staying through the summer to nest,
you may find it possible to interest a farmer, your hunting part-
ners, your school teacher, or local bird club, in planting aquatic
vegetation suitable for your area.

Before you attempt or even plan such a project, you would be wise to consult your local game warden, Soil Conservation Service, or the United States Bureau of Sport Fisheries and Wildlife. They can supply you with the necessary basic information you need on aquatic vegetation, the types best adapted to your locale, and the best planting techniques. Planting aquatic vegetation for wild-fowl can be a most disappointing venture, and one can easily be discouraged unless the advice of professionals is sought. All of these agencies gladly offer advice and information, and with their help your planting project has a much better chance of successful development.

Planting trees, shrubs, and thickets for windbreaks and cover along fence lines is a good conservation project in rural areas to provide for upland game birds such as pheasants and quail. In the northern states, pheasants especially need protective cover in the winter. Just a small patch of evergreens or willows, planted in thick stands, will develop quickly and form a welcome refuge for many birds. Pheasants are especially vulnerable to heavy snow-storms and bitter cold winds. Unless they have adequate shelter, many birds perish through the long winter.

If you develop some shelters for pheasants, you will also enjoy keeping some feed available when the snow is deep. This is a practice that many sportsmen have followed for years in the northern states. It pays off in a better bird crop the following fall. Many state conservation departments cooperate in these programs by supplying individuals and groups with suitable tree seedlings for windbreak and cover planting. The trees are usually made available at very low cost. Game wardens and conservation officers are always ready and willing to help any person or group interest-ed in shelter planting.

Waterfowl can usually be attracted to newly created nesting grounds without resorting to stocking, if suitable cover, food, and nesting sites are developed. How soon this happens would depend on such factors as predators, hunters, abundance of water through-out the nesting season, and the number of breeding birds in the area. Once the ducks or geese accept your nesting grounds, many of the young hatched there will return the following spring. If no breeding birds seem to be frequenting your area, you could enlist the help of your conservation department. Ask for a few pairs of restocking birds to start with in the early spring. Or you can pur-chase breeding stock from a game farm.

Probably the most enjoyable undertaking of all is establishing "instant nesting" habitat for ducks and geese. It is amazing what strange devices can be successfully employed as nesting habitat for

232

waterfowl. Old tractor tires, washtubs, oil drums, treetop platforms, hay bales, and packing boxes are just some of the odd innovations that have induced geese and ducks to nest in areas where little or no waterfowl population has existed for years, if ever. All you need is an old abandoned sandpit, sewage lagoon, cow pasture pond, or swamp. Almost any place that retains water through the nesting season and provides sufficient cover and vegetation for feed will do.

In recent years there has been increasing interest in providing instant nesting habitat for waterfowl throughout the country. Honkers have been lured into unlikely nesting places in Missouri, using the washtub nest idea. In Maryland, the Canadas have been quite content to incubate their eggs in old tractor tires placed beside small pasture ponds. Mallards are delighted to move into old oil drums with the top and bottom knocked out and mounted horizontally on platforms over the water.

It is necessary to supply nesting material for these instant habitat sites. Hay, straw, reeds, wood chips, or dry grass can be used to fill the nests. It is important to have the material at the site when the birds arrive. They will arrange the material to suit, but if it is there and easily available on the nest when they come, the appeal is all the stronger, and you are more likely to have a pair or two move in. The Bureau of Sport Fisheries and Wildlife, Washington, D. C., is one excellent source for information on planning and constructing instant nesting habitat. You can also obtain helpful bulletins on this subject from the Superintendent of Documents, Washington, D. C.

The tree-nesting wood duck is one of our most widely distributed waterfowl, but in many areas it has difficulty finding suitable nesting trees. Wood ducks have been forced to give up in some areas where fire, logging, and land development have destroyed large tracts of woodlands. You may find that by erecting some nest boxes near a lake or stream in your area you can encourage wood ducks to nest there. The "woody" will readily accept a properly made box as a substitute for the natural tree cavities which it uses. And it will return to your box year after year. This is a proj-

MALLARD AND CANADA GEESE
By Bob Hines—U.S. Dept. of Interior, Fish and Wildlife Service

ect anybody can undertake quite easily and at very little expense. It is not difficult to build a wood duck nest box, but it is essential that it have the proper design and location.

The Agriculture Extension Service of Pennsylvania State University has published an excellent bulletin on how to construct and erect a wood duck nest box. Following are portions quoted from the bulletin, including illustrated plans:

"Building nest boxes for wood ducks is a fine individual or club project. The boxes can be built in home workshops, school shops, or on the farm. Spring field trips to erect the boxes and subsequent checking will often result in unusual observations of the shy and wary wood duck. You will certainly receive a great deal of personal satisfaction in knowing that 'woodies' are using your nest box.

"Don't count your wood ducks before they are hatched. Studies have shown that large nesting losses occur in these man-made boxes. Raccoons, in some areas, are most serious offenders in egg stealing, but squirrels, crows, and snakes sometimes develop the habit of robbing wood duck nests. To prevent such losses, a box that would exclude raccoons was designed. The plans shown here illustrate how to build an inexpensive and durable nest box. The eliptical shaped hole is designed to prevent the raccoon from entering. This is an important feature that should be closely followed in cutting the hole.

"Nest boxes should be erected by April 1 (in Pennsylvania) in order to be available to the 'woodies' when they arrive on their spring migration. Location of the boxes should be near bodies of water such as lakes, beaver dams, streams, or farm ponds. Desirable nest box locations are most often found adjacent to or over the water, so it is best to take advantage of these situations when possible. Boxes can often be erected during winter months when ice permits walking on the pond. Where squirrels are abundant, it is desirable to place the boxes on poles or snags surrounded by water.

"Fasten the box to a sturdy, sound tree, snag, or pole which is located in the open. See that the entrance hole is exposed and plainly visible. Avoid overhanging limbs and branches which would make it difficult for the duck to find or enter the box. It is not necessary to use a perch or landing platform on the box, since wood ducks enter the hole from a full flight. This indicates the importance of having

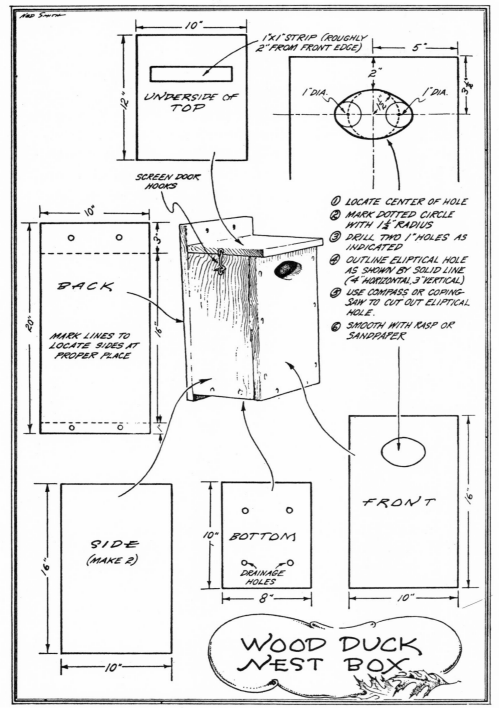

UNDERSIDE OF TOP

1"x1" STRIP (ROUGHLY 2" FROM FRONT EDGE)

10"

12"

5"

2"

1" DIA.   1" DIA.

3½"

SCREEN DOOR HOOKS

① LOCATE CENTER OF HOLE
② MARK DOTTED CIRCLE WITH 1½" RADIUS
③ DRILL TWO 1" HOLES AS INDICATED
④ OUTLINE ELIPTICAL HOLE AS SHOWN BY SOLID LINE (4" HORIZONTAL, 3" VERTICAL)
⑤ USE COMPASS OR COPING SAW TO CUT OUT ELIPTICAL HOLE.
⑥ SMOOTH WITH RASP OR SANDPAPER

BACK

MARK LINES TO LOCATE SIDES AT PROPER PLACE

10"

20"

3"

16"

SIDE (MAKE 2)

16"

10"

BOTTOM

DRAINAGE HOLES

10"

8"

FRONT

16"

10"

WOOD DUCK NEST BOX

—Courtesy of Cooperative Extension Service, College of Agriculture, The Pennsylvania State University

plenty of clearance for the duck's approach. Use a heavy spike lag bolt or galvanized wire to fasten the box in a secure position out of reach of high spring water. It is a good idea to consider a convenient height, since it will be necessary for you to have access to the box for later checking. Four or five feet above the water level is satisfactory.

235

"It is important to place two or three inches of dry wood shavings in the bottom of each box. Wood ducks will seldom accept these artificial nesting sites without this natural nesting material. This factor alone probably accounts for the failure of wood ducks to use many boxes.

"Maintenance of wood duck boxes is necessary. Yearly checks should be made before April to remove old nesting litter and replace it with dry shavings, when necessary. Owls, squirrels, starlings, and bees may establish themselves in boxes intended for wood ducks. Remove old nests and debris left by these visitors."

Most conservation officers recommend cypress as the best wood for the nest box. Pine may be used, but should be surface treated with a preservative to delay rotting. One important feature to include is a three-inch strip of screen tacked on the inside of the box leading from the bottom to the entrance hole. The young ducklings will use this as a ladder to climb to the hole when they are ready to leave the nest. If the box is smooth inside, they will not be able to climb out.

Attracting wildfowl is a fascinating experience that anybody can participate in one way or another. If you can't do it alone, join a group or organization that is involved with wildlife or conservation. If you have a sincere interest in improving wildfowl habitat in your community, look around you for the most likely places. The place you find may seem very unlikely, but if it has water, food, and cover, the birds may find it acceptable when you have made the necessary adjustments and provisions. Even one solitary wood duck nest box can be a good start. In almost every community there is something that an individual or a group can accomplish in making that area more attractive to some species of wildfowl.

OUT FOR AN AIRING (CANADA GEESE)
By Bob Hines—U.S. Dept. of Interior, Fish and Wildlife Service

BIRD BANDING
—TRACING THE WANDERERS

As a young duck hunter in far-off Peru picks up the blue-winged teal he has just shot, he notices a bright metal band on the bird's leg. Removing the tiny aluminum strip, he reads the inscription stamped on it: "Advise Fish & Wildlife Service, 656-24378. Write Washington, D. C., U.S.A." A week later the band arrives in the mail at the Bird Banding Laboratory of the Patuxent Wildlife Research Center, Laurel, Maryland. In the same mail is a similar band from a bird watcher in Ecuador who found a blue-winged teal on a lakeshore, victim of a fatal gunshot wound. Both bands tell the Banding Laboratory a fascinating history of these two migratory waterfowl. From its highly sophisticated computerized records, the laboratory staff quickly determines that the teal in Peru was banded six months earlier by a U.S. game management agent in Saskatchewan, Canada. Thus the story unfolds. This little teal had flapped its way for seven thousand miles — over a dozen international boundaries — in that time. The teal in Ecuador, the records revealed, had been banded at the Delta refuge in Manitoba, Canada.

The band from a pintail duck taken by a hunter near the city of New Mexico revealed that this bird had been banded thirteen years before at the Bear River refuge in Utah. At that time, this was an old-age record.

Another interesting waterfowl travelogue was told by a pintail banded at the Bear River refuge. The bird and the band were recovered eighty-two days later at Palmyra Island, eleven hundred miles south of Honolulu. The pintail had made an overwater flight of more than three thousand miles!

The banding of birds for scientific study was started in 1899 by a Danish schoolteacher, Hans Mortensen, who first banded white storks. His work stirred the interest of other Europeans, and soon there were many banding operations in progress throughout Europe. It spread to the United States, and in 1909 the American Bird Banding Association was formed for the benefit of organizations and individuals engaged in banding work. As the importance of these programs became more evident,

RING-NECKED DUCKS
By Bob Hines—U.S. Dept. of Interior,
Fish and Wildlife Service

the work was transferred to the Bureau of Biological Survey in 1920. In later years, banding has been officially supervised by the U.S. Fish & Wildlife Service.

Millions of birds of many species have been banded over the years through the cooperation of many organizations and individuals. However, with a few exceptions, waterfowl are banded only by biologists and game management agents in the refuges throughout the northern hemisphere. The banding program is no longer done haphazardly, as was the case when it first began. It is now programmed carefully, according to the specific types of information needed for each species.

Biologists of the Migratory Bird Population Station at the Patuxent Wildlife Research Center know precisely what banding information is already on file for each species. And they know the most urgent needs for additional data. They assign "quotas" of waterfowl to be banded at specified times of the year in various parts of the continent. Then state, federal, and Canadian biologists begin the required tagging. All official banding in North America is part of one coordinated system. This greatly simplifies record keeping, which now covers more than eleven million birds, four million of which are waterfowl. About half of the six hundred thousand birds banded each year are waterfowl. And about four-fifths of the band recoveries each year, which average about forty thousand, are waterfowl.

Banding not only indicates the migration habits of waterfowl species, but it also provides biologists with a wealth of valuable and useful information for planning better management of waterfowl and conservation of their water resources and habitat. The data helps determine the value of particular breeding grounds in supplying ducks and geese to specific hunting areas. It reveals variations in total hunting pressure from year to year in the different sections of the country. It shows losses in population due to hunting, disease, lead poisoning, and predation. It indicates sex and age, mortality, longevity, and the period during which the population of any given year continues to provide hunting. Banding is an excellent index of the total annual kill of waterfowl.

All this data is collected by means of the recovered bands and compiled in elaborate statistical records by computers. It is then available for immediate reference at the Patuxent Bird Banding Laboratory, which is the central collecting agency for the entire North American banding program. When a recovered band is received, the banding laboratory staff, in a matter of minutes, can assemble the complete information on the banded bird. Anyone who sends in a band is notified of the date and the location where it was placed upon its bearer.

The recoveries of bands come from far and near. They are reported by people in all walks of life — hunters, bird watchers, hikers, campers, fishermen, farmers, aircraft pilots, and workmen who find birds and waterfowl killed by telephone and electric power lines, tall buildings, and other structures into which migrating birds fly at night. Bands come from Indians in the jungles of South America and Eskimos of the subarctic regions. Many of the mysteries concerning where certain species of birds winter and nest have been solved in recent years through the information supplied by recovered bands.

Ingenious methods are used for capturing waterfowl to be banded. Geese are often trapped while feeding on dry land, by means of a long, folded net that is swiftly projected over the unsuspecting birds by the thrust of several small camouflaged cannons that shoot the net up and over the geese before they can escape. When the geese flock to an area baited with corn, this system easily captures a large number. The net settles over them gently, causing no harm. The netted birds are immediately banded and released. Young geese may be shipped to another refuge in an effort to re-establish a species in a region where it once nested.

Many ducks are trapped for banding simply by luring them into a chicken-wire cage, with a funnel entrance baited with barley and wheat.

Another method is to drive large numbers of surface-feeding ducks into net corrals erected near shore. This is done when the birds are in their annual molt and cannot fly. A crew of men, in canoes or wading in shallow water, drive the birds before them into the corral. This method works fine for the surface-feeders, but not so well for the diving ducks, which can dive under and by-pass the canoes and drivers.

A rather startling new way for tracking birds and waterfowl is to color them with bright dyes. This idea was first used by the California Fish and Game Department in 1955 to check on the northbound goose flight. Immediate evidence of its value was forthcoming as astonished observers phoned in reports of pink, green, and yellow geese all the way up to the Arctic Ocean. This method has limitations. When the birds molt, the colored feathers are shed that same summer.

The continued success of the international banding program depends to a large extent on the teamwork of sportsmen, naturalists, and administrators. Hunters throughout the continent have been most cooperative in reporting recovered bands from waterfowl and other game birds. Hopefully, they — and all others — will consider this to be a part of their responsibility as hunters and citizens to aid in the continuation of their sport and the future of all waterfowl.

FIGHT FOR SURVIVAL (SCAUP)
By Bob Hines—U.S. Dept. of Interior, Fish and Wildlife Service

HOW FAST AND HOW HIGH
DO THEY FLY?

In the chill gray dawn, a duck hunter scrunches down in his blind as he spots a small flock of pintails far down the lake. Hoping they may swing over his decoys, he checks his gun and waits. As the birds pass near a point, still far away, they suddenly flare, and seconds later the boom-boom of gunshots comes rolling across the water, as hunters blaze away without success. Now thoroughly frightened, the pintails turn on more speed. They wheel and come straight for the hunter's blind. But they're still high. He guesses they are only going to buzz his blocks and will not turn and come in. So he quickly decides to chance a shot as they go over. Here they come — moving with incredible speed! He swings his gun up and around, well ahead of the lead duck, and fires. Misses! As he watches them disappear, he wonders just how fast they were flying. He guesses at least one hundred miles per hour. But he is wrong, as most hunters are when estimating the speed of ducks after throwing a couple of futile shots. A more realistic guess would be sixty miles an hour — perhaps less. Pintails have been clocked at sixty-five when chased by planes, and this seems to be about their top speed.

The matter of the speed at which birds can fly is a controversial subject, especially among sportsmen, who are inclined to greatly overestimate the speed at which ducks, geese, and other game birds fly. There are very few game birds of any kind that can fly more than sixty miles an hour. Two of these are the canvasback duck and the pintail.

Few game birds develop an air speed of more than sixty miles an hour by their own effort, without the aid of a tailwind. Sportsmen, of course, are judging the ground speed, which is the velocity of the actual progress of the bird, either accelerated or retarded by the influence of the wind and other atmospheric conditions. Air speed is the rate at which a bird moves through the air by its own effort, without regard for any influence of the wind. However, air speed of birds is difficult to measure, although it would be a more accurate comparison of birds' capabilities than ground-speed measurements.

Most birds have two flight speeds, their normal flight and their escape flight, which for some birds can be nearly double their normal rate of speed. They increase their speed simply by flapping faster. The size and shape of the wings in comparison to the weight of the bird are factors that determine its speed of flight. Birds with small wings in proportion to their weight require more speed to maintain flight, and their wingbeats are more rapid than those of birds with larger wings. The mallard and the canvasback are good examples. The wing surface of the slower-flying mallard is about 20 percent greater than that of the swifter canvasback. The canvasback compensates for this smaller supporting surface by more rapid wingbeats and its streamlined form, which reduces air resistance.

A popular misconception is that the smaller game birds — teal for instance — are faster than the larger birds. This is a false impression due to the smaller bird's fast rise and take-off. The heavier birds are generally conceded by ornithologists to be faster, once they are airborne. Mallards can usually outfly teal when pursued or frightened, although many hunters believe teal are the speediest of the ducks, with the exception of the canvasback. Probably it is the teal's small size that gives this impression.

More reliable data on the speed of bird flight has been gathered in recent years, with the aid of scientific equipment. It is now quite generally accepted that the usual flying speed of ducks and geese is between forty and fifty miles an hour. For smaller birds it is much less.

There are always exceptions, however. The common loon is an example of a large bird with relatively small, primitive wings that can fly very swiftly. Loons have been clocked at fifty-three and sixty-two miles an hour. One loon was timed in a shallow dive while pursued by an airplane at ninety miles an hour and was steadily pulling away from the plane.

Old squaw ducks have been accurately timed over measured courses at 54, 61.5 and 72.5 miles an hour with 11-mile-an-hour tailwinds.

Wood ducks in Wisconsin have been timed at forty-six miles an hour on a windless day. The fastest wood-duck time recorded is fifty-five miles an hour.

Through the willows (Mallards)

The following chart lists some recorded speeds of wildfowl, gathered from various sources, and is a fair representation of the data currently available:

Canvasback	72 m.p.h. air speed, chased
Pintail	65 m.p.h. air speed, chased
Mallard	46, 50, 55, 60 m.p.h. air speeds
Shoveler	53 m.p.h. ground speed
Goldeneye	50 m.p.h. ground speed
Redhead	42 m.p.h. ground speed
Old squaw	54, 61.5, 72.5 m.p.h., 11 m.p.h. tail wind
Wood duck	46, 55 m.p.h.
Cinnamon teal	59 m.p.h., chased
Prairie chicken	42 m.p.h.
Wild turkey	35 to 42 m.p.h.
Woodcock	35 m.p.h.
Canada goose	60 m.p.h., air speed, chased
Whistling swan	50 to 55 m.p.h. air speed
Cackling goose	45 to 48 m.p.h. ground speed
Brant	45 m.p.h. air speed
Snow goose	50 m.p.h. air speed, chased

243

How high do they fly?

The scientific observations of the flight altitudes at which birds and wildfowl migrate have improved in recent years with the development of radar. The original observations were, of necessity, estimates made from the ground. Today, with the aid of radar and high altitude aircraft, the study of bird flight altitude has been greatly expanded. These more recent studies reveal birds flying at amazing altitudes, hitherto thought impossible for many of the small birds. A catbird was struck by a plane above the cloud level at thirty-seven hundred feet, an unusual height for a bird that spends most of its time near the ground. But since it was spring, the catbird was apparently migrating. Ducks have been seen by aircraft pilots as high as eighty-five hundred feet, and swans at eight thousand feet. Shore birds have been observed at twenty thousand feet flying past Mount Everest in India. But these altitudes are probably unusual and do not indicate the normal migratory flight of most birds.

It is believed that 90 percent of the birds migrate at night, including the waterfowl, and that the greater part of migration takes place below three thousand feet above the earth's surface. And much of this is at less than one thousand feet, which would usually be below the cloud level, where most birds seem to prefer to fly.

At dawn (Mallards)

THE HELPING HANDS

Much of the progress that has been achieved in saving our wild-fowl from total extinction must be credited to the unselfish and enthusiastic work of organizations dedicated to preserving our nation's resources.

As individuals, most of us are limited in what we can accomplish alone to improve the general welfare of wildfowl. But when we combine our efforts with thousands of others who share our interests, we are then able to generate a powerful and influential force for good. The banding together of those with love for living things has created many useful groups that have an immeasurable effect upon public thinking. Each of these organizations has its place in the national conservation picture. Each is important in educating, legislating, constructing, and sponsoring wildlife conservation projects. All such associations deserve the endorsement and financial support of the entire nation. Most of us who have any interest at all in our great outdoors and its wildlife are associated in some way with one or more of these groups. But there are many who are not sharing in these endeavors. In the hope that some may decide to merge their interests with a worthy group, we will briefly review here the activities of various public-spirited organizations that are leading the way in wildlife conservation.

Ducks Unlimited

Surely one of the foremost guardians of our wildfowl heritage is the rather unusual organization known as Ducks Unlimited— unusual because much of its work in behalf of ducks and geese is done outside the United States in the prairie provinces of Canada, where about 80 percent of the North American duck population is produced. The basic purpose of Ducks Unlimited is to preserve the wetlands in the Canadian breeding grounds and to guarantee a continuing control over the water supply that is so vital to propagation of waterfowl in the prairie provinces. Their efforts have been magnificently successful. It is quite likely that if this international brotherhood of dedicated duck hunters had not gone into action some thirty years ago, when waterfowl population was at its lowest ebb, the battle for survival of both ducks and geese would have been lost years ago.

No public funds are used to finance the many projects sponsored by Ducks Unlimited. Since its founding in 1937, the organization has depended entirely on the contributions of American and Canadian sportsmen to finance the program. Well over nineteen million dollars have been contributed in the three decades that Ducks Unlimited has been active.

The major work of Ducks Unlimited has been concerned with obtaining long-term leases on existing or potential wetlands from private and public landholders. Then water control structures are created to maintain proper and constant levels. This long-range, permanent control program is now working effectively at nine hundred project areas, re-establishing them as prime breeding grounds, and guaranteeing them as productive locales for future waterfowl generations.

All the land Ducks Unlimited supervises is made available by individual farmers and by the Canadian government, under long-term, no-cost lease. No land is purchased. Thus every dollar goes into construction and maintenance rather than land purchase. This has resulted in one million six hundred thousand acres of prime waterfowl nesting habitat built or restored, and over eight thousand miles of vital protective shoreline created or stabilized. Hundreds of thousands of ducks and geese have been banded by Ducks Unlimited workers. And thousands of acres of waterfowl food has been planted.

This is one group that has clearly demonstrated, in the American tradition, what can be done in conservation of wildlife when a well directed and concerted effort is made. National headquarters for Ducks Unlimited is in Chicago — Post Office Box 66300, Chicago, Illinois 60666.

The Izaak Walton League

"Defenders of soil, woods, waters, and wildlife." That is the noble slogan and battle cry under which the Izaak Walton League of America has marched since 1922. This is another organization that has a long record of direct action designed to preserve and protect our many wonderful resources, including the air we breathe.

One of the first major achievements of the "Ike Waltons" was its influence in the establishment of the three-hundred-thousand-acre Upper Mississippi Refuge for fish and wildlife. It was through the League's efforts that Congress appropriated funds for the establishment of this important national refuge.

It was the Izaak Walton League that saved the starving elk herd in Jackson Hole, Wyoming, years ago and was influential in establishing the National Elk Refuge there. Over the years, the Waltonians have been in the forefront in obtaining the establishment of numerous major refuges throughout the United States. It

Lake Erie Mallards

has an outstanding record in its fight against stream pollution. The League's influence has been instrumental in cleaning up many streams and rivers where pollution from industrial and municipal wastes were destroying wildlife.

The Izaak Walton League numbers its members in the many thousands, most of whom are ordinary fishermen, hunters, and lovers of the outdoors, who make annual membership contributions to finance the League's work.

The accomplishments of the Izaak Walton League are far too numerous to relate. It has lived up to its slogan and by its actions has effectively achieved many of the principles it proclaims. It is a dynamic group that has demonstrated not only the need for conservation, but also has initiated the action to get the job done. Much of the League's efforts presently are concerned with river and air pollution, pesticides, and other forms of pollution that are making our major rivers sick and totally unfit for wildlife and recreation. National headquarters are at 1326 Waukegan Road, Glenview, Illinois 60025.

The National Association of Audubon Societies

Every school child is familiar with the Audubon Society and its educational programs used in classrooms and Audubon Junior Clubs. The society is the first major conservation group organized in the United States, dating back to 1886. Of all the conservation groups, the Audubon Society has undoubtedly had the most profound effect upon the American public's attitude toward birds and wildlife in general. Many game bird hunters have been prone to condemn the Society, claiming that Audubon members are complete protectionists and if they had their way would abolish all hunting of waterfowl. This, of course, is entirely untrue. The Audubon Society asks only that there be reasonable and adequate restraints, and insists that the waterfowl resource must be provided capable and effective management. The Audubon Society's philosophy is to consider the interests of the birds first, the hunters second. And we know that this is the only philosophy that can assure the perpetuation of our magnificent legacy of birds and wildfowl.

But like most of the conservation groups, the Audubon Society does not confine its interests solely to birds and waterfowl. Many of its major activities are centered on conserving all our natural resources, and it devotes a considerable amount of its energy to arousing the public to a greater awareness of the perils that threaten our resources and our very existence.

Local Audubon Societies thrive in almost every community throughout the nation. Members come from every walk of life, but all have a common and devoted interest in birds, waterfowl, and all forms of wildlife and natural resources. Junior clubs abound and are an important institution for teaching young people to love, respect, and cherish our great heritage.

Through the years great changes have been brought about in protective measures to save various species of birds and wildlife, and much of this change has been due to the influence of the Audubon Society. It has established and maintained wildlife sanctuaries and materially aided in their patrol. Audubon wardens patrol millions of acres of land and water. Some are deputized by federal and state governments to enforce wildlife laws and regulations. When the early Audubon Societies were trying to fight the destruction of birds for millinery feathers, two Audubon wardens were shot and killed by poachers. Today, Audubon wardens teach thousands of school children the intricate wonders of nature and lead parties of visitors through the society's many sanctuaries.

The Audubon Society also maintains four Audubon centers — in Greenwich, Connecticut; Sharon, Connecticut; Dayton, Ohio; and El Monte, California. The centers are used to train teachers and youth leaders through personal experiences with nature. A more recent program, the Nature Centers Program, promotes the creation of community-owned-and-operated areas for nature study by school children and youth organizations. The Society provides technical assistance in planning and organizing the centers.

In addition to a wealth of intensely interesting literature and books, the Society publishes a magnificent magazine for its members. National headquarters are at 1130 Fifth Avenue, New York, N. Y. 10028.

National Wildlife Federation

When President Franklin D. Roosevelt called the first North American Wildlife Conference in Washington, D. C., in 1936, there evolved from that historic meeting a non-profit corporation known as the National Wildlife Federation. One of the proclaimed purposes of the conference was to focus attention upon the many social and economic values that wildlife has for our people. The Federation was formed to disseminate pertinent facts, discoveries, and information relating to the preservation and restoration of wildlife through the conservation of soils, waters, plants, and forests. The Federation today is said to be the world's largest private conservation organization, representing two million Americans interested in the wise use and protection of our natural resources.

The Wildlife Federation is an excellent source of educational material for teachers and students. The Federation participates in teachers' workshops and conferences, provides educational material for scouts and youth groups, distributes more than five hundred thousand pieces of educational literature annually on a free or nominal-cost basis, and sponsors world-wide safaris for the study and enjoyment of wildlife and natural beauty. It also cooperates with women's clubs, garden clubs, and sportsmen's organizations. Financial grants are made each year to assist graduate students in conservation courses and in research efforts.

In addition to the wealth of high quality literature published and distributed by the Federation, it publishes a superb magazine in full color, *National Wildlife,* and an auxiliary publication of equal quality, *International Wildlife.* It also sponsors the popular Ranger Rick's Nature Club for young people and publishes the colorful *Ranger Rick's Nature Magazine* for members.

Anyone with an interest in nature study, wildlife, and conservation should be encouraged to utilize the extensive services and helpful materials being made available by the Federation. A membership in this group is an excellent investment. The national office of the National Wildlife Federation is at 1412 16th Street, N. W., Washington, D. C.

Other Organizations

The roster of distinguished organizations that are making significant contributions to conservation in America today is an impressive one.

The Wildlife Management Institute is one of our very important national groups whose efforts are producing splendid results in many fields of conservation — waterfowl in particular.

The National Geographic Society contributes substantially to our knowledge of wildlife and conservation and sponsors numerous research and scientific study projects related to various conservation needs.

The Sierra Club is vitally concerned with our environmental problems and is one of the dependable watchdogs over our valued resources in the rivers, lakes, and forests, and all forms of wildlife. The influence of this organization is being felt today wherever a strong voice is needed to speak up for action.

Outdoor Writers Association of America's members are professional journalists, writing extensively on hunting, fishing, and outdoor news, — outspoken reporters who are conservation-minded. They seek by their activities and writing to make worthwhile contributions to conservation and preservation of our wildlife and other resources, and the teaching of better sportsmanship in all recreational journeyings into the outdoors with dog and gun, or rod and reel. This group is an effective force in molding public conservation opinion.

The Wilderness Society ranks among the top organizations engaged in the conservation battle.

The Society of American Foresters, American Ornithologists' Union, the American Nature Association, and the American Society of Mammalogists are but a few of the many organizations that have done much and are continuing to further the work of conservation. All are helpful and needed in our struggle to restore and protect wildlife and improve our total environment.

The helping hands in the cause of wildfowl include countless small clubs and individuals who are carrying on conservation projects of many kinds to maintain our wildfowl. Thousands of hunting clubs are doing excellent work in providing refuge areas for waterfowl.

There is a place and a need for every one of us who cherishes the land and its great heritage of wildlife. It is our personal responsibility to find our niche and become active. Everybody should pay for conservation. It benefits everyone, so why should not everyone share in the financing? The bird watchers, hikers, wildlife photographers, wildflower enthusiasts, mushroom and blueberry pickers — all have the same stake in this great outdoor and wildlife heritage. We can no longer expect the hunters' and fishermen's money to pay the cost of saving our wildlife.

CAN THEY SURVIVE
OUR ONRUSHING CIVILIZATION?

What is the future of our wildfowl? Will the struggle for survival be won or lost? The prospect is anything but encouraging. In our rapidly eroding environment total extinction now threatens every form of life, including mankind. What happens to the wildfowl and other wildlife will be determined by how willing we are to give a high priority to the basic action that must be taken.

Greed, apathy, and indifference to essential values have put us on a collision course with ecological disaster. And by every measurement we are losing ground. Our air is dirtier. Our water is more polluted. Our land—for food, wildlife, and living space—is degenerating. Vital minerals may soon be exhausted. The outlook is frightening, if not downright desperate.

The long-range problem is competition for land and water between wildfowl and civilization, with its increasing population. The tragic aspect of this situation is that if it comes to a final showdown and the wildfowl habitat—both land and water—is needed to produce food and living space for the expanding population of mankind, the wildfowl will lose out. And that will be the beginning of the end for them. If that comes to pass, nothing can save the wildfowl.

Man himself has created the problem. Millions of acres of prime wildlife habitat have been undergoing destruction since this country was settled by the pioneers moving westward. This was inevitable. But the wildfowl tenaciously hung on and adapted as best they could. Their numbers have continued to dwindle, and nothing can ever bring them back to their original status, when their flocks darkened the skies like black clouds.

Now, the habitat situation is in a critical state. It is estimated that each year a million and a half acres of prime wildlife habitat are being taken for highways, airports, housing, and industry. Year after year we drain more swamps or flood them by damming streams. More land is reclaimed for marginal agricultural operations. All this development takes desperately needed land away from wildlife. Federal, state, and local governments are attempt-

252

Lucky pond (Mallards)
Reproduced by permission of Richard E. Bishop

ing to set aside more refuges and reservations for wildlife living space. But the acres lost still outstrip those that are being saved.

A federal acquisition program to preserve substantial areas of wetlands and vital wildfowl production habitat is necessary. But such a program faces extreme difficulty. Competition for these lands by other interests is certain to thwart possible acquisitions. Land prices will soar out of reach. And much desirable land will be converted to other uses before any acquisition program can take action. Furthermore, the high priority demands for water, in many areas across the country, will prevent securing needed water rights for waterfowl use. These are serious problems with which we now must cope. They will grow far more serious as the relentless pressures of civilization increase.

Sad to say, it is the waterfowl — ducks and geese — that are in the gravest danger. Despite the fact that they lay large clutches and recover quickly from disaster if given a chance, waterfowl face a dubious future. Unlike pheasant, quail, and grouse, that can spread themselves over millions of acres, waterfowl must concentrate where the water is. They must contend with not only the swamp drainers and land grabbers who deprive them of water, but also with drought and floods which through the years have brought disaster to the waterfowl in many of the principal breeding grounds. And to this we can add the heavy toll taken by hunters. It is amazing that migratory waterfowl have done as well as they have, considering the obstacles to their normal way of life that have resulted from man's ever-expanding needs.

What about pollution? Even though we may secure sufficient wildfowl habitat to maintain a stable bird population, will we lose it to the menace of the many forms of chemical pollution that are now ravaging our waters and soil? This is a possibility. Dr. George Wallace, a pioneer in the study of the effect of DDT on songbirds, predicted that unless we call a halt, "we shall have been witnesses, within a single decade, to a greater extermination of animal life than in all the previous years of man's history on earth."

The increasing use of pesticides and herbicides may prove to be the most serious threat yet to all wildlife. Some of our finest rivers and lakes have already felt the killing effects of DDT, mercury, and other destructive chemicals. Some of our most highly prized birds, including our national symbol, the eagle, are now endangered species, unable to propagate normally due to the effects of poisonous pesticides deposited in fish and other food they consume.

It is entirely possible that we could be successful in acquiring enough suitable habitat to sustain our wildfowl, only to lose them in the battle against pollution. It is a fearful prospect, because it is not only the birds that will perish. When wildlife is endangered by a poisoned environment, so is man.

Perhaps the future of wildlife, and waterfowl in particular, lies in scientific research. Not that research can solve all the problems. But there are some areas in which more knowledge and better technology could overcome wildfowl production deficiencies. Assuming that in the future we will have set aside enough habitat to support a population, it may be possible for research to provide practical methods for maintaining and even increasing that population on the relatively limited habitat space available. For example, research may find ways to encourage more breeding pairs to nest on the suitable areas available—two, three, or four nesting pairs where only one would normally nest. This would produce a larger population on less habitat. There are game management people who believe it can be done. Research may also discover how to reduce the high mortality rate of waterfowl at the egg and duckling stage. Even a slight improvement here would result in a substantial increase in waterfowl. Research may also develop a method for producing and raising to maturity all species of wildfowl artificially, in the same manner that fish are propagated in fish hatcheries. This would assure a stable bird population, easily controlled.

There is no swift, sure way to overcome the tragic dilemma that threatens our existence and that of every living creature around us. But the most important force, above all others, that will save wildlife and us, is *us*. As someone recently said, "We have met the enemy and he is us!" We are indeed the enemy— the polluters and the devastators who have brought calamity down upon ourselves and life in every form. We cannot escape the indictment. We have been ignorant of, or indifferent to, sound ecological practices. We remain selfish, and apathetic to the terrible desecration in which each of us is participating. Nothing will be accomplished to clean up our polluted world until we—you and I—get to work undoing the damage where action is needed.

There may be hope. The human race is showing a new awareness that there will surely be a miserable and diminishing style of life unless it has the good sense to reverse the destructive conditions infecting its way of life. The danger is now apparent.

One hopeful sign! People are talking—still somewhat vaguely—about *ecology*—a term previously recognized by only scholars and specialists in the field (meaning the branch of biology dealing with the relation of living things to their environment and to each other). A balanced ecology is absolutely necessary if mankind and his world are to survive.

Some people reason that the technology which landed men on the moon can and will correct our environmental problems. But technicians agree that it is easier to shoot a man to the moon than to clean up New York City. There seems to be no clear-cut idea of what we — as a nation and as individuals — should be doing, or how we should do it. Some are aroused — some are worried! But not enough are fighting mad or frantically eager to save our nation, or our wildlife, from what is almost certain extinction.

There is so little time in which to choose what kind of existence we will have in the future — or what kind of relationship we will have with our land, our water, our air and our wild creatures. The compelling question is, will we awaken to the terrifying reality of it all and choose wisely, before time runs out?

COMMON GOLDENEYE HEN AND BROOD
By Bob Hines—U.S. Dept. of Interior, Fish and Wildlife Service

Index

Numbers in italics refer to illustrations